BEDS & BORDERS

fine Gardening

BEDS & BORDERS

DESIGN IDEAS *for* GARDENS LARGE AND SMALL

FROM THE EDITORS & CONTRIBUTORS
OF *FINE GARDENING*

The Taunton Press

The Taunton Press
Inspiration for hands-on living®

The Taunton Press, Inc.,
63 South Main Street, PO Box 5506
Newtown, CT 06470-5506
e-mail: tp@taunton.com

Editor: Renee I. Neiger
Developmental editor: Jennifer Renjilian Morris
Copy editor: Candace B. Levy
Indexer: Jay Kreider
Cover design: Kimberly Adis
Interior design: Kimberly Adis
Layout: carol singer | notice design

Fine Gardening® is a trademark of The Taunton Press, Inc., registered in the U.S. Patent and Trademark Office.

The following names/manufacturers appearing in Fine Gardening *Beds & Borders* are trademarks: Accent® White impatiens, Black & Decker®, Diabolo® ninebark, Canna Tropicanna®, Edge Hog®, Emperor I® Japanese maple, Festival Grass™ burgundy cordyline, Fourth of July™ rose, Knock Out® rose, Magic Carpet® spirea, Margaritaville™ yucca, Meidiland®, Perennial Plant Association®, Plant of the Year™, Sunny Delight® euonymus, Roundup®

LIBRARY OF CONGRESS CATALOGING-IN-PUBLICATION DATA
Fine gardening beds & borders : design ideas for gardens large and small / from the editors and contributors of Fine gardening.
    p. cm.
Fine gardening beds and borders
Beds and borders
Design ideas for gardens large and small
Includes index.
ISBN 978-1-60085-822-2
1. Beds (Gardens) 2. Garden borders. 3. Landscape gardening. I. Fine gardening. II. Title: Fine gardening beds and borders. III. Title: Beds and borders. IV. Title: Design ideas for gardens large and small.
SB423.7.F56 2012
635--dc23
                    2012028908

PRINTED IN THE UNITED STATES OF AMERICA
10 9 8 7 6 5 4 3 2

ACKNOWLEDGMENTS

Thanks to the many contributors—authors, photographers, illustrators, and editors—to Fine Gardening *magazine. Thanks to the book's editors: Jennifer Renjilian Morris, for all of her hard work putting this book together, and Renee I. Neiger, for overseeing the project.*

CONTENTS

INTRODUCTION

I WILL ALWAYS REMEMBER THE FIRST BORDER I EVER CREATED.
It was about 10 ft. long and about 2 ft. deep, but I cut an edge
for it that looked like it was done by a chipmunk who'd had a few
espressos. It went in and out, zigged then zagged, and curled back
in on itself before exploding out again in another arc. All this was,
as I said, over the course of about 10 ft. I had read that curves
made beds and borders more interesting, and that was what I was
going for. I thought my edge was the coolest thing around—until I
tried to mow along it.

The overall silliness of my edge dawned on me gradually. And
while the advice about curves and interest is sound, it isn't the
only way to approach shaping a bed or border. As you read this
book, you will get plenty of advice from experts; some of it will
apply to you, some won't. But you should still pay attention to the
parts you think you can skip. There are principles there that still
apply to the successful creation of beds and borders. So read, plan,
and plant—just take it easy on the curves.

Steve Aitken, Editor, Fine Gardening

BASICS

Difficult landscape conditions were embraced when locating plantings, paths, and pools in the Abkhazi garden.

✓ **DESIGN IDEAS**
✓ **HOW-TO**
✓ **LANDSCAPE SOLUTIONS**
✓ **NATURAL LANDSCAPE**

❁

MAKE THE MOST
OF WHAT YOU'VE GOT

Successful gardens aren't made in a day. Peggy and Nicholas Abkhazi spent years observing their site before creating gardens that reflect the landscape's beauty and terrain. Professional landscaper Daryl Beyers shares the lessons learned from their labor of love.

GOOD GARDENS, LIKE GARDEN DESIGNERS, ARE NOT BORN OF nothing. They grow from the observation of opportunities that present themselves over time. By learning to embrace what is best in a landscape and responding well to whatever challenges are there, a garden plan has every chance of success. When I first saw the Abkhazi garden in Victoria, British Columbia, I was in awe. Impressed by the mature beauty exhibited by a garden 60 years in the making, I looked around and recognized a design developed through observation and thoughtful decisions. This process, which I have taught to garden-design students, places time at the heart of design.

Time makes landscape gardening a dynamic endeavor. It is also what gives gardeners their sense of power: the power to shape life and land beyond the scope of ordinary ages. When a seedling stick from a plastic pot grows into a towering mass of branches and leaves, its roots spreading deep in the ground, the dimension of time in a garden is plain to see—though often only in photos or memory.

Nestled into the garden at the end of the long lawn, the summerhouse fits into the landscape like a natural feature and provides views to the rest of the garden.

Peggy and Nicholas Abkhazi had learned the lessons of time before they began building their garden. Their youth was cut short by personal tragedies suffered during World War II, and they rebuilt their lives by focusing their creative energies on a 1-acre lot near the southeastern tip of Vancouver Island in Canada. There, they patiently used time to observe, embrace, and respond to their landscape. The result of this long labor of love is a garden that demonstrates a sense of belonging with the land on which it was made.

OBSERVE BEFORE YOU DESIGN

In 1946, the Abkhazis' discreet lot was nothing more than an unused strip of ground. Where others saw a difficult terrain covered with immovable glacial rock, the Abkhazis envisioned something special. The couple would arrive every morning from a house they rented nearby, and after putting a kettle on a camp stove in a small summerhouse (see the photo at above) Nicholas and Peggy studied their

landscape. Through the seasons of an entire year, they observed their sloped land cut diagonally along hard lines of exposed rock, studying the changes in weather, wind, and sun.

Good garden designers first observe and study their site to discover its strengths and weaknesses. A thoughtful designer will recognize and record important existing features of the landscape in a sketch called a *site survey* (see the drawing on the facing page) which includes basic landscape features such as the sun's orientation, or aspect (which way is north?); the shape, size, and quality of significant landforms (including hills, slopes, low spots, and bodies of water); and the type and tilth of the soil.

Second, a useful site-survey sketch will describe every plant or planting bed on the property. This is the first step in distinguishing between trees with positive potential and those that will distract from the design. Other questions to ask at this stage are whether any established herbaceous plantings are worthwhile, and if there is turf, does it grow well or struggle to survive?

Third, map all man-made structures on the property. The location of the main house, outbuildings, walls, and walks will determine how they can be included in any proposed garden spaces. Also, make note of existing fences, decks, and patios.

Finally, recognize and record less-tangible qualities of the site, such as views that expand the garden's horizons or comfort spots where it simply feels good to be. Spaces that encourage activity stand out as candidates for areas to play or entertain, while uncomfortable areas call out for improvements. Deciphering these intangible qualities will influence crucial design decisions throughout the making of your garden.

EMBRACE WHAT IS GOOD ABOUT YOUR SITE

Every landscape, large or small, possesses distinctive characteristics that give it personality. The Abkhazis recognized the beauty and interest of their difficult terrain and decided early on to turn these apparent limitations into strengths.

Glacial-rock formations highlight the landscape, and the Abkhazis featured them in the plan by building their garden alongside, as well as within, the unyielding rock (see the photo at right). Every line of design they created was drawn in harmony with the timeless flow of the rock formations. The shape of plantings, paths, and open areas all emulated the unique geological features. For example, the branch patterns of recumbent conifers echo the flowing lines of the rock formations on which they stand.

Nicholas and Peggy also chose to create a place to view the garden from within a grove of native garry oaks (*Quercus garryana*, USDA Hardiness Zones 7–9), whose potential they recognized during their patient observation of the site. Sixty years later, fully mature trees and the glacial landforms in which they reside impart a palpable sense of ecological continuity and faithfulness to the original landscape.

Many gardens are unique due to their landform. Steep slopes, open fields, or running water are all features one can embrace within a design. For example, one can build pocket terraces along a hillside or frame a view toward a lake.

By incorporating the imposing outcrop into the design, the Abkhazis created a seamless transition between house and garden.

SITE SURVEY

A colored map that shows key existing features, such as landforms, structures, plants, and views, is critical as you begin to decide what to keep and what to change.

- Property line, driveway, roads
- Landforms
- Plants
- Structures
- Attractive views

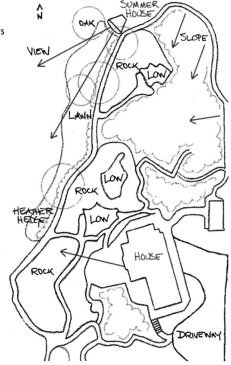

Look for the same values in preexisting plants, primarily trees. If a property is surrounded by a pine forest, then embrace the forest and build a plant palette that will thrive in the understory.

As for structures, don't consider that tumble-down, dry-stack stone wall as just a pile of rocks. Rather, see it as a piece of geographic history (or a handy source of edging stones). Whatever the case, it is important to recognize the value of all preexisting features of a landscape.

RESPOND TO WHAT NATURE PROVIDES

The existing landscape also dictated what the Abkhazis added to their site. They laid a path from the south lawn to the summerhouse by following the contour at the base of the rock formations and then lined it with a heather hedge (see the top photo on the facing page). The two elements together create a natural walkway to

TOP Follow the natural lines drawn by land contours when locating lawns, borders, and pathways.

RIGHT Expand your spaces by creating stopping points and moments of interest with steps, landings, and terraces built on a hillside.

the summerhouse and form a textural buffer between the rough stone and the soft grass. A natural curve is one of the most difficult lines a designer can draw, but by following the contour of the glacial arrangement, this path assumes a legitimate, natural form.

Another design dilemma is the proper placement of water features. The Abkhazis took advantage of large depressions where water collected naturally to create their reflective pools. The ponds are placed perfectly because they respond to what the terrain offered.

Over the years, plants were established on the rock formations wherever a trowel might probe and roots take hold. Certain species thrived and remained, whereas others failed and were forgotten. It was not a gardener's whim that selected the plants seen there today but a natural course of succession.

The best reason to observe and respond to a landscape is that it makes for happier gardening. Accomplished gardeners roll with the punches. If, after a rain shower, water fills the front lawn, perhaps a bog garden is in order. The lesson and legacy of the Abkhazi garden is never to fight nature. It is wiser to accept what it offers and take advantage of what it allows.

TOP Weave a tapestry of flowers and foliage by building pockets of good soil into difficult locations.

ABOVE Grow the plants that like your conditions, such as this rock rose (*Helianthemum* cv., Zones 6–8), thyme (*Thymus* sp., Zones 4–9), and dianthus (*Dianthus amurensis*, Zones 3–9) both chosen for hardiness in lean soils.

✓ ADD COLOR
✓ DESIGN IDEAS
✓ HARDSCAPES
✓ HOW-TO

CREATE UNITY
IN THE GARDEN

With so many gorgeous plants to choose from, it can be difficult to figure out which ones will work best in your yard. Northwest gardener Cindy Stockett has devised three unifying elements to keep in mind when shopping so you can buy the plants you love and still keep your garden feeling connected.

IF YOU GARDEN, YOU LOVE PLANTS—ESPECIALLY THE NEWEST and most unusual ones. After bringing these treasures home, they often end up plopped in various places without a lot of preplanning or design in mind. And as the number of trips to the nursery increases, so does the number of planting plots, leaving many of us with a series of smaller beds around our property that have no real connection to one another. Although these gardens are filled with many treasures, they have no sense of continuity. This can happen in any garden, regardless of its size.

Small or large, gardens need unifying features to tie one area to the next and to create a sense of flow. Without that stability, things can get wild and out of control, making you feel uneasy and unsure of where to look or where to walk. Faced with this problem in my own yard, I came up with a three-part solution to help blend my entire landscape together.

Keep potential chaos in check. Make a clear, cohesive connection between several smaller gardens by using a common color, establishing a signature plant, and incorporating water throughout.

ESTABLISH A BACKBONE PLANT

To help pull my landscape together, I chose one hardy, fairly basic shrub and used it as a backbone plant throughout the garden. Because the backbone plant is such an important part of the garden's framework, careful thought should be given to its selection. Your backbone plant should be evergreen because it needs to be seen in all seasons. And, above all else, it needs to be low maintenance: It shouldn't require frequent spraying or pruning because your time should be spent on maintaining the rest of your garden. Shrubs, rather than perennials, work best as backbone plants because they are

large enough to have a noticeable presence in the garden but won't dominate the scene as focal points.

In my Pacific Northwest yard, 'Winter Gem' dwarf boxwood (*Buxus microphylla* var. *japonica* 'Winter Gem', USDA Hardiness Zones 6–9) was the perfect backbone-plant choice because it fit the essential criteria. The consistent use of this dwarf shrub establishes order in my garden beds, especially where there is an abundance of various perennials. The boxwood is like green hardscaping, drawing the eye forward as you move through the garden because it is a repetitive and recognizable element.

ABOVE and RIGHT Boxwood is the ultimate backbone. Because it is evergreen, is low maintenance, and has a distinct presence, 'Winter Gem' boxwood is the perfect signature plant for this garden (above). Its tidy, compact form also helps define the lines of the beds (right).

INTEGRATE AND REPEAT A COLOR

No matter what the size of your garden, it is important to choose a color or color combination and repeat it to help unify the entire landscape. I often use combinations of burgundy and blue, which is a striking pair of contrasting colors. Some of my favorite perennials to use in this color scheme are Festival Grass™ burgundy cordyline (*Cordyline* 'Jurred', Zones 9–11), 'Britt Marie Crawford' ligularia (*Ligularia dentata* 'Britt Marie Crawford', Zones 4–8), and 'Pacific Giants Mix' delphinium (*Delphinium* 'Pacific Giants Mix', Zones 3–7). Whatever combination you choose, make sure it has bold contrast that catches and holds the eye. Good pairings include chartreuse and burgundy, yellow and blue, and burgundy and pink.

To further the sense of continuity, you should also incorporate large trees and shrubs that have your repeated color. This strategy works well in small gardens, and it is essential in large gardens because extra space gives the eye more room to get lost. To repeat my burgundy theme, I incorporated into my larger space purple smoke bush (*Cotinus coggygria* cv., Zones 5–9), Diabolo® ninebark (*Physocarpus opulifolius* 'Monlo', Zones 3–7), and 'Royal Cloak' Japanese barberry (*Berberis thunbergii* 'Royal Cloak', Zones 5–8). Although our property is several acres, you still feel as if you were in the same garden anywhere you stand thanks to these large splashes of familiar color.

It can be frustrating to go to the nursery with a well-thought-out and researched plant list and not be able to find what you are looking for. Instead of a specific

BELOW In every garden, architectural features need to relate consistently to each other, either by style or color. If they don't, they not only stick out like sore thumbs but also separate a space instead of uniting it. I chose the triangle peak of my house as the inspiration for my gates, pergolas, and archways to the garden areas.

plant list, draw up a set of criteria that fits the spot you are hoping to fill: for instance, a large plant (size) that is chartreuse (color) and is round (shape). This will give you more options and more success in finding plants that will help you achieve your goal.

CREATE FLOW WITH WATER

Water is an important element in any garden. It can drown out traffic noise, create a sense of serenity, attract birds, and create movement. But it can also be a wonderfully simple way to introduce commonality to a space. Water appears in many forms throughout my gardens. I have large features, like ponds and fountains,

BELOW A repetitive color combination should offer a pair of bold, contrasting hues because they draw your attention and leave a lasting impression. The combination of chartreuse and burgundy—as seen in the leaves of the golden Japanese forest grass (*Hakonechloa macra 'Aureola'*, Zones 5–9) and the blooms of 'Hadspen Blood' astrantia (*Astrantia major 'Hadspen Blood'*, Zones 4–8)—works well together.

but I also have small-scale pots filled with water plants that I place in smaller beds. Water features in various places in the garden act as bold unifiers, not only for their visual presence but also for the sound they provide.

Many gardeners shy away from installing water features because they are afraid of the maintenance. But I have never installed a single water garden that couldn't take care of itself. I use bundles of barley straw (available at garden centers and online) to help reduce algae in ponds because they work as an organic filtering system. I also use mosquito dunks that contain Bt (*Bacillus thuringiensis*) to control mosquitoes in standing water features. The installation and minimal maintenance of these features are well worth it when you see and hear how water brings your space together.

Gardening is a personal and creative form of expression. Your garden should reflect your taste and should not be bound by someone else's rules. It is important, nevertheless, to consider and consistently apply guidelines that help create an outdoor space that flows and feels unified. After all, the goal is to create a garden that is more than just a collection of plants; it's a continuous and complementary space that everyone—including you—can enjoy.

TOP Create curves. A good garden layout is essential for giving your space continuity and for developing a sense of flow. Instead of simply lining up plants like soldiers against a wall, use curved bed lines to encourage the eye forward to the next space and to keep the garden from being revealed all at once.

ABOVE Don't be intimidated by water features. It's easy to incorporate water into the garden on a large or a small scale. Anyone can add a simple pond-in-a-pot, and even a small waterfall can be low maintenance.

✓ **DESIGN IDEAS**
✓ **LANDSCAPE SOLUTIONS**
✓ **PLANT SUGGESTIONS**

SPONTANEOUS DESIGN

Sometimes meticulous planning works best, and sometimes you just need to let your imagination run wild. Garden writer and designer Steve Silk inspires you to get out into the garden and wing it.

I LOVE MAKING PLANS FOR MY GARDEN—BUT NOT ON PAPER. My most rewarding design efforts take place as I'm daydreaming. I gaze about the garden and imagine what I'd like to see. I think about the lines of its paths and beds, the interplay of plants, and the juxtaposition of shapes, textures, and colors. Hours of such seeming inactivity suddenly yield fruit—an "Aha!" moment that opens the sluice gates of my creativity. Now I know the perfect spot for that new 'Sky Pencil' holly. It'll look great rising alongside the red dome of a Japanese maple.

Though my approach to design may seem unorthodox, I suspect it's shared by many. I view garden making as an evolving process rather than as the pursuit of a fixed idea (aka a plan on paper). My fluid, ongoing method is as flexible as it gets. I simply remember that nothing need be permanent and that it's interesting and usually easy to change things. I'm often not quite sure where my efforts are leading, and I don't really care. I'm trying new plants and new ideas, and I'm having fun. I'm open to changing conditions, flashes of inspiration, and sudden whims. Every garden-design problem has many solutions, and exploring the possibilities excites me. I keep refining my vision of my garden, and its beds and borders look better every season.

In your imagination, any combination is possible. Don't be afraid to play with ideas before putting plans to paper.

On the whole, I'm not worried about making mistakes. That's because, as a friend once pointed out, making a mistake just gives you the chance to do a little more gardening. Nonetheless, there are several techniques I use to support and hone my intuitive design process.

USE VISUAL AIDS

One thing I've discovered is that you cannot design in a vacuum. You need to do something that helps you get a rough impression, in advance, for how a completed project will look. I start as simply as possible.

PLAY WITH SHAPES BEFORE MAKING THEM PERMANENT

Before laying out a new bed within a lawn area, start playing with its shape. Each time you mow the lawn, leave the site for the potential bed unmown. Then you can tweak its rough outlines by simply altering the path of the mower. Once you have a rough approximation that you like, further refine its perimeter lines using a garden hose or rope to outline the bed (see the left photo below). When using a hose, I let the sun warm it so that it's soft and pliable.

A variation on this technique works for siting paths as well. Again, within a lawn area, I let the grass get a little long. Then, in subsequent mowings, I use the mower to create paths of varying shapes and widths so that I get a good idea of what will make a pleasing pattern. Where there's no lawn to mow, I define the edges of paths by using a garden hose, stakes, or slender trunks or branches of fallen trees lined along the ground.

USE ANNUALS AS STAND-INS

A good way to preview long-term projects is to use stand-ins. If you're thinking of planting a hedge or making a divider in the garden, plant a row of fast-growing annual castor beans (*Ricinus communis* and cvs.), which rapidly create a dense wall of foliage at least 5 feet tall (see the top photo on the facing page). This helps you visualize how

LEFT and ABOVE Before you break ground with an edger, test out your shape with a garden hose. Once you have the line you want, dig in and put down your edging.

a hedge will look. You can use the same technique to get a feel for how a tree or large shrub might look in a given spot. For example, I used a castor bean plant as a preview before planting an empress tree (*Paulownia tomentosa*, USDA Hardiness Zones 5–8).

ASK YOUR FRIENDS TO ACT AS SHRUBS

Pieces of lumber and a few garden tools are also useful to visualize effects or to calculate spacing. You might jab a pitchfork or shovel in an evolving part of the garden to get a rough sense of the relative size and proximity of trees and shrubs. Sometimes I press friends into service and have them hold a piece of 2×4 lumber in place or just stand with their arms outspread as I evaluate the placement from different vantage points.

DON'T HESITATE TO MOVE WOODY PLANTS

Woody plants are not immune to my passion for plant shuffling. Because I'm often uncertain about how to use a plant that's new to me or my garden, I regularly end up moving woodies at least once before I find them a good home. I moved a Japanese maple (*Acer palmatum* var. *dissectum*, Zones 5–8) a few times before settling on a spot at the head of a long, narrow bed. There, its burgundy dome provides a soft, smooth entry point for the eye. It looks even better backed by the narrow spire of a 'Sky Pencil' holly (*Ilex crenata* 'Sky Pencil', Zones 5–7), which also lived at several addresses before taking up its present residence.

TOP Tall annuals can be used as a placeholder while you test out size and shape. If you like it, then plant the perennial you want for the space.

ABOVE Sometimes you need help visualizing how much space a large plant will actually take up. A willing friend can act as a stand-in while you step back and take note of the space.

Woody plants can be transplanted if you change your mind about their placement.

ABOVE A simple pruning can do wonders for the overall dimensions of your garden. Don't overlook this option when you're analyzing your site.

LEFT Sometimes you just get lucky and find a combination that works completely by accident.

TAKE AN INTERACTIVE APPROACH

Because change is at the heart of gardening, planting design is an ongoing process for me. In my garden, many—if not most—plants have been moved at least once. Keeping my plants on the go allows me to divide perennials regularly and to keep pace with my evolving understanding of my garden's microclimates and, more important, my sense of garden style.

DON'T BE AFRAID TO PRUNE

Some trees simply must be cut down to size. Seven-son flower (*Heptacodium miconioides*, Zones 6–9) is often the subject of rave reviews, so I had to try one. It grew rapidly and filled its allotted space quickly. Despite its great fall flowers, however, I found the plant rangy and chaotic looking. So I cut it to the ground so that it would come back as a lower, denser shrub. I'll continue to coppice it from now on. Coppicing enables me to grow other trees that would otherwise be too big for their intended place; the list includes smoke bushes (*Cotinus* spp. and cvs., Zones 4–8), golden-leaved catalpa (*Catalpa bignonioides* 'Aurea', Zones 5–9), elderberries (*Sambucus* spp. and cvs., Zones 3–9), several willows (*Salix* spp. and cvs., Zones 4–9), empress tree, and large hydrangeas (*Hydrangea paniculata* and cvs., Zones 4–8, and *H. macrophylla* and cvs., Zones 6–9).

IF SOMETHING WORKS, DO MORE OF IT

I'm always trying plants, whether they're hot new introductions or pass-along plants from gardening friends. I plant them in several places and in different combinations to see how they perform. During this phase, I do a lot of moving and dividing. Those that take off are then planted in abundance. I take special delight in finding and using plants that perform against type, as it frees me to make unexpected combinations. I like *Hosta* 'Royal Standard' (Zones 3–8) not just because it's fragrant; I was pleased to discover that, unlike most hostas, it also thrives in full sun. And I've got a planting of golden groundsel (*Ligularia dentata* 'Othello', Zones 4–8) in a spot that's theoretically too sunny for this lover of shade and moisture.

Annuals sometimes yield surprises, too. I'm keen on large-leaved plants for full sun. They're invaluable for adding hefty substance to sunny borders, which often look a little fluffy because most sun lovers have small or linear foliage. When I first happened upon cannas (*Canna* spp. and cvs., Zones 8–11), I planted a few of them at intervals along the borders. I was so taken by their bold effect that my passion for plants took a sudden sharp turn toward the tropics. Thanks to that chance purchase, I now grow all kinds of large architectural annuals for the punchy sense of structure they provide.

MAKE THE MOST OF SERENDIPITY

I often find inspiration in happenstance, like when I discover a dynamic combination in randomly placed plants or come up with a scheme for whatever plants or objects I have on hand. In the garden, unpredictability is a wonderful asset.

TAKE ADVANTAGE OF HAPPY ACCIDENTS AND WINDFALLS

Sometimes success comes by accident and you should be open to it. While consolidating a bunch of plants in a nursery area near my garden, I discovered that my seed-grown kale and a six-pack of an annual sage made great textural counterpoints and shared a similar color (see the bottom photo on the facing page). I quickly made plans to plant a whole drift, backed by a sprawl of ornamental purple millet (*Pennisetum glaucum* 'Purple Majesty').

I've dug up countless rocks in the making of my garden. Early on, I used them as edging for my raised beds because it was easier than carting the stuff away. Now I edge all my beds with fieldstone. The rock serves as a unifying element and adds to the sense of place I've tried to create. When I unearth a boulder with a particularly interesting shape or color, I turn it into an impromptu ornament, like a miniature standing stone (see the left photo on the facing page).

TEST A NEW PLANT BEFORE DECIDING ON A HOME

I'm always open to pass-along plants, plants from some can't-pass-it-up sale, or plants accorded "latest and greatest" status by preeminent plants people, which makes them instant must-haves in my book. One day, I snatched up a golden meadowsweet (*Filipendula ulmaria* 'Aurea', Zones 3–9) when I found it on sale. I brought it home and promptly started the plant dance—cha-cha-chaing around the garden, new plant in hand, trying to find it just the right spot.

I don't always find new plants a home right away. So I keep a nursery area that is usually well stocked with seedlings, divisions, and other new plants. After all, it's nice to have a few plants at the ready—another design inspiration might strike me at any moment.

ABOVE Even though it's located in a sunny spot, my shade-loving golden groundsel happily self-sowed nearby, so I took the hint and planted more.

RIGHT Try out different locations while plants are still in pots.

Low-growing blue rug juniper (Juniperus horizontalis 'Wiltonii') gracefully mingles with selections of sedum and silver mound artemisia.

❋

MASS PLANTINGS
MAKE A BOLD STATEMENT

When gardening expert Ruth Adams bought her new home, a renovated barn with a large backyard, she needed a garden that stood out among its surroundings. By grouping masses of just a few plants, she created the harmony and impact she was looking for and now you can do the same.

I LEARNED ABOUT THE VALUE OF MASS PLANTINGS WHEN MY husband and I bought a renovated barn with a large backyard opening to a 3-acre hay field. I liked the fact that our site enjoyed full sun and a magnificent view of mountains, but I was stumped initially by this new gardening challenge. I knew that traditional English perennial beds would not suit the architecture of the barnlike house and that a cottage garden would be dwarfed by the vista.

So I turned to some principles of Japanese gardening. I tried to identify with the pervading spirit of the site, use its strengths, and, most of all, remain sensitive to the existing scale. Given our location, it made sense to place the garden between the expansive view and the house. Mass plantings of low-growing plants seemed the best way to achieve harmony between the garden and the surrounding landscape. These plantings complement, rather than compete with, the natural panorama and can be enjoyed both close up and from a distance. Well-placed mass plantings in any setting can draw the eye and lend a naturalistic air to a garden.

Repetition of a single plant can create a sense of unity. Masses of blue oat grass are repeated throughout the garden.

EVALUATE THE ROLE OF MASS IN YOUR LANDSCAPE

In gardening terms, *mass* refers to a body of coherent plantings, usually of indefinite shape and often of considerable size. It can be created by grouping several pots of the same plant or several plants that have similar color, texture, and density. For example, two or three plants that bloom at the same time in a similar color can form a mass. Or several varieties of grasses—even of varying heights—can be combined to make a bold statement.

Because mass is a relative term, it must be developed in relation to other elements—architectural structures, other plantings (such as a shrub hedge), or even open lawn. Looking at the surroundings of my future garden helped in determining an appropriate sense of scale.

First, I considered the ratio of the proposed garden (when viewed from the house or terrace) to the imposing backdrop of field, forest, and mountain range. Thinking "big," I tried to balance the massive scale of the site by breaking up the sloping, rectangular lawn with a 50-foot by 70-foot pond. This also solved the dilemma of what to do with a gaping hole filled with several huge boulders left behind by the previous owners. We moved the rocks and placed them around the pond.

This became a perfect setting for massed plantings. For example, around the side of the pond closest to the house, I planted only low-growing junipers (*Juniperus* spp.) and cotoneasters (*Cotoneaster* spp.). Viewed from a distance, these plantings appear as broad sweeps.

KEEP MASSES IN PROPORTION

Proportion is key to determining how many plants to mass in an area. For example, in a spot roughly 100 square feet on the far side of the pond, I planted clusters of four different plants—two varieties of *Sedum*, silver mound artemisia (*Artemisia schmidtiana*), and snow-in-summer (*Cerastium tomentosum*). The effect of these combined forms, textures, and colors is akin to the muted shadings of a tapestry (see the photo on p. 24).

I alternated these ground-cover masses with low-growing focal points: standards of *Juniperus procumbens*

'Nana' and weeping trees such as Norway spruce (*Picea abies* 'Pendula'), katsura tree (*Cercidyphyllum japonicum* f. *pendulum*), and Eastern hemlock (*Tsuga canadensis* 'Pendula'). They add height and definition to the planting area's boundaries.

I've also found that smaller gardens, or smaller spaces in large gardens, can usually handle some massing of plants. In a walk-in bed behind the pond—about 10 feet wide by 35 feet long—I planted drifts of colorful perennials that draw the eye through the path (see the photo below right). As a general rule, I used not fewer than 5 pots of the same perennial in a section, and in most cases I used 7 to 13. I made exceptions for big plants, such as *Nepeta* 'Six Hills Giant' and *Crambe cordifolia*. The number of plants I choose, and how I group them, is ultimately determined by eye. Whenever possible, I opt for a naturalistic, flowing style.

In keeping with the open-field style of the landscape, I included prairie plants such as coneflowers (*Echinacea* spp.), bee balms (*Monarda* spp.), and monkshoods (*Aconitum* spp.) punctuated with blue oat grass (*Helictotrichon sempervirens*). I especially like the hedgelike effect created by a band of black-eyed Susans (*Rudbeckia fulgida* var. *sullivantii* 'Goldsturm') backed by a dwarf fountain grass (*Pennisetum alopecuroides* 'Hameln').

ABOVE Space plants to allow for mature growth. The author lays out a large bed of heaths and heathers in which she interspersed a few juniper and cypress plants.

RIGHT Plant perennials in groups of five or more for eye-catching appeal. This bed features masses of balloon flowers (*Platycodon grandiflorus*), blazing stars (*Liatris spicata*), and black-eyed Susans.

USE MASSES TO ACCENTUATE COLOR OR TEXTURE

When planting in masses, the goal is to see broad sweeps rather than insignificant patches of color and texture. Many low-growing perennials look appealing en masse. For example, groupings of plants with textured foliage, such as junipers, heaths (*Erica* spp.), and heathers (*Calluna vulgaris*) make excellent foundation plantings when informal, curving lines are desired. And spreaders like dead nettle (*Lamium maculatum* 'White Nancy') and wild ginger (*Asarum canadense*) are wonderful ground covers beneath trees.

Taller plants can help create a balanced sense of scale along with groupings of shorter perennials. For prairie-style screens or see-through hedges, mass tall native plants such as Joe Pye weed (*Eupatorium fistulosum* 'Gateway') in combinations with grasses such as species of *Miscanthus*. For a dramatic effect in a woodland area, group large numbers of ostrich ferns (*Matteuccia struthiopteris*), Japanese painted ferns (*Athyrium niponicum*), or hostas.

Lackluster plantings, especially shrubs, also can become the basis for creating a mass. One way is to simply plant more of an existing plant or type of plant. For example,

a spindly row of lilacs can be transformed into a billowy cloud of color and scent by adding new plants among the established ones. For shrub masses that offer fall and winter interest, plant large clusters of Japanese hollies (*Ilex crenata*) or Sawara false cypress (*Chamaecyparis pisifera*).

I also create drifts by filling in spaces between existing plants. I designed a hot border on one side of the lawn by using a spotty arrangement of a dozen or so peonies (*Paeonia* spp.) as the backdrop for sweeps of plants with foliage or blooms in shades of deep red, yellow, and white.

USE ANNUALS AS FILLERS

It's often difficult to create a finished-looking garden while waiting for plants to mature. Massing annuals around slower-growing plants is a simple way to overcome this challenge. Statuesque plants like *Nicotiana sylvestris* can add sculptural shapes until new shrubs mature. Ground-hugging annuals will fill in gaps between newly planted perennials and, if they self-seed, can contribute elements of unpredictability and excitement year after year. Given the ever-increasing selections of annuals available, it's easy to find suitable companions. And, because perennial gardens often lose their luster in the dog days of summer, planting annuals can be a perfect way to perk up the beds. It's fun to experiment with annuals because the presentation can always be changed the following year.

ABOVE Create a hedge with two dense layers of perennials: here, a row of black-eyed Susans is backed by dwarf fountain grass.

RIGHT Accentuate colorful foliage plants by growing them en masse. A ribbon of purple sage (*Salvia officinalis* 'Purpurascens') makes an attractive edging.

WEAVE A GARDEN
WITH GEOMETRY AND COLOR

Creating continuity in the garden is a dilemma, and many people struggle with it. Fortunately, garden designer Barbara Blossom Ashmun has three foolproof strategies that will pull together a wide array of garden beds.

MANY OF MY STUDENTS AND DESIGN CLIENTS LOVE THE DIVERSITY that flowering trees, shrubs, and perennials offer but have trouble linking their garden beds to each other—a trick that makes the whole picture flow gracefully. Frustrated with a hodgepodge of colors and textures, they ask me for tips to help them pull their garden design together. In some cases, we've even dug up all the plants in a border, placed them on a large tarp, reorganized them into more pleasing combinations, and replanted. Over the years, I've come up with three helpful strategies to transform collections of individual plants, both on a small and large scale, into harmoniously arranged compositions.

Pick a theme and use it consistently. The author chose to make all her beds curved, and their similar outlines create a feeling of unity. Dozens of tulips scattered throughout the beds also provide a connection.

ABOVE The use of circular objects, such as a round umbrella, reinforces the curves of the beds.

RIGHT Repeated groupings of lady's-mantle, bloody cranesbill, 'Husker Red' penstemon, and 'Mozart' rose lead the eye through this border.

GEOMETRIC SHAPES CREATE A SENSE OF CONTINUITY

By taking a shape that already exists in the architecture of your home or landscape and repeating it in your beds and borders, you can create a sense of continuity throughout your garden. For example, if the shape of your patio is rectangular, straight paths would echo the lines of the patio. Square or rectangular garden benches and planter boxes could be used as complements. That is not to say that shapes unrelated to your home or landscape design can't work. They can. Just pick a theme, and use it consistently.

In my garden, most of the beds are oval or circular; their similar outlines create a feeling of familiarity and unity. The rounded beds have curved paths surrounding them in a natural geometry. I've repeated these curved lines and shapes by placing a round picnic table, shaded

by an umbrella, and surrounding it with curved benches nearby (see the left photo on p. 32).

Similarly, when I chose a greenhouse for my garden, I couldn't resist the round, spaceshiplike Sturdi-built Sunflare. Round birdbaths and terra-cotta pots echo this circular theme. To support climbing roses and honeysuckle, I built curved arbors. And someday I hope to have curved pergolas like the ones in Monet's garden.

WAVES OF COLOR DRAW THE EYE FROM ONE AREA TO THE NEXT

I think of a border as a sandwich; the front and back sections are like bread, and the middle of the border is the filling. If the bread is substantial enough, it will hold a lot of filling. When the edges and backs of your borders are generously filled with waves of the same color, whether from flowers or leaves, you can get away with a lot of variety in the middle of the border and the picture will still look orderly.

In sunny borders, I rely on the yellow blooms of low-growing lady's-mantle (*Alchemilla mollis*, USDA Hardiness Zones 4–7) and the magenta flowers of bloody cranesbill (*Geranium sanguineum*, Zones 4–8) for sweeps of color along the bed's edge. In the middle of the plantings, 'Husker Red' penstemon (*Penstemon digitalis* 'Husker Red', Zones 2–8) stands at attention, displaying clouds of pinkish white blooms atop its maroon stems. Sometimes nature helps out too, by seeding drifts of annuals like blue Spanish love-in-a-mist (*Nigella hispanica*) or purple *Verbena bonariensis*, and all I have to do is cull out the excess.

Colorful leaves serve the same unifying purpose and last even longer than flowers, usually from early spring through late fall. I like to combine the contrasting duo 'Chocolate Ruffles' coralbells (*Heuchera micrantha* 'Chocolate Ruffles', Zones 4–8) and lamb's ears (*Stachys byzantina*, Zones 4–8) in areas that receive no more than a half day of sun. In deep shade, either an edging of golden Japanese forest grass (*Hakonechloa macra* 'Aureola', Zones 5–9), blue 'Halcyon' hosta (*Hosta* 'Halcyon', Zones 3–8), or silver-leafed 'Excalibur' lungwort (*Pulmonaria* 'Excalibur', Zones 4–8) will provide a punchy accent.

Shrubs with colorful leaves can be used to line the backs of beds. The best shrubs for this are those that can be pruned each year, which keeps their foliage fresh and their size manageable. Be daring: Try the wine-colored leaves of 'Diabolo' ninebark (*Physocarpus opulifolius* 'Diabolo', Zones 3–7), 'Royal Purple' smoke tree (*Cotinus coggygria* 'Royal Purple', Zones 5–8), or 'Guincho Purple' elderberry (*Sambucus nigra* 'Guincho Purple', Zones 6–8) in areas with full sun to partial shade. In darker corners, let the golden leaves of 'Sutherland Gold' cutleaf elderberry (*Sambucus racemosa* 'Sutherland Gold', Zones 3–7) or golden ninebark (*Physocarpus opulifolius* 'Luteus', Zones 3–7) glow. The bright yellow foliage of 'Briant Rubidor' weigela (*Weigela* 'Briant Rubidor', Zones 4–9) also makes a glimmering backdrop for shady borders.

Once your garden matures, it's even easier to pull it together. Look around and select your favorite perennials, such as the ones with good foliage that also bloom for a long time. Divide and distribute them throughout the garden so that they become the links among your beds.

REPEAT PLANTS WITH BOLD FORMS TO CREATE VISUAL CONTINUITY

Whether you are working with a large or a small garden space, repeating a few signature plants will create visual continuity throughout a series of beds. These can be the same plants or ones that resemble one another, such as perennials with similarly tinted flowers or those with similarly colored leaves. Try repeating leaves with a dissected or grassy form or flower shapes like spikes, disks, or globes. You can also focus on echoing plants with a similar habit like mounded, upright, or arching, which will bring the design together when viewed from a distance.

To tie one long bed together, I repeated clumps of horizontally striped zebra grass (*Miscanthus sinensis* 'Zebrinus', Zones 4–9). These tall beauties look great among late-blooming sedums (*Sedum* spp. and cvs., Zones 3–10), yellow coneflowers (*Rudbeckia* spp. and cvs, Zones 3–9), and Joe-Pye weeds (*Eupatorium* spp. and cvs., Zones 3–9), especially when they are backlit by the afternoon sun.

One fall, I potted up a dozen containers of wine- and pink-colored tulips (*Tulipa* 'Attila' and *Tulipa* 'Toyota', Zones 4–8) that were scheduled to bloom in April. Placing several pots in each of three island beds, I tucked them between the leaves of low-growing leafy shrubs such as *Senecio* 'Sunshine' (Zones 9–10) and *Abelia* 'Confetti' (Zones 6–9) so that the pots were hidden and the tulips bloomed above the foliage. They made vibrant splashes

Continuity within a bed is created by repeating bold shapes, such as the upright and eye-catching zebra grass.

of the same color from bed to bed, turning lonely islands into a friendly archipelago (see the photo on p. 30).

The same effect can be accomplished by repeating blossoms with similar colors and forms. I like to place the blue flower spikes of speedwells (*Veronica spicata* cvs., Zones 3–8) and larkspur (*Delphinium* cvs., Zones 3–7) in sunny, unrelated areas to provide a common thread. In shady places, try repeating pockets of the tiny, lavender-pink, pompon-shaped blooms of 'Hewitt's Double' meadow rue (*Thalictrum delavayi* 'Hewitt's Double', Zones 5–9) and the light pink, cup-shaped flowers of 'Max Vogel' Japanese windflower (*Anemone × hybrida* 'Max Vogel', Zones 4–8). Even though they have differing flower forms,

their similar colors can be used to unite garden beds in late summer and fall.

Sprinkling white flowers through several beds is also a riveting way to relate them to each other because white draws attention. I planted white cranesbills (*Geranium sanguineum* 'Album', Zones 4–8) in a sunny island bed, white calla lilies (*Zantedeschia aethiopica*, Zones 8–10) in a neighboring shady island, and a white 'Doctor Robert Korns' rose (*Rosa* 'Doctor Robert Korns', Zones 5–8) in a nearby border to tie all three areas together (see the photo on p. 32).

Two towering shade trees can't stop this garden from glowing. Light abounds in the form of bright green and vibrant yellow foliage.

❋

LOVE YOUR SHADE

Just because your property is shady doesn't mean you have to give up on having a beautiful garden. Using a few simple tricks, garden designer Scott Endres helps you transform any dim spot into the highlight of your garden with these bright ideas.

MOST OF US AREN'T FORTUNATE ENOUGH TO HAVE A FULL DAY'S worth of sun in our gardens, yet even the most experienced among us is still a little intimidated by shady areas. They're often uncharted territory—the last place you want to plant because you're not even sure what will grow there. But there are plenty of options that can bring light and life to your dark space. Simply remember that a successful shade garden starts with good plant choices.

When you begin exploring your plant options, you'll discover a plethora of textures and forms. You'll also find plenty of color—most notably, shades of green and light-simulating chartreuse and silver. The first step is to pair these plants, focusing on establishing contrast among textures, shapes, sizes, and colors to help you play up the qualities of each plant. Next, become aware of how the plant combinations work in relation to the scale of their environment, how they create focal interest, and how they draw the eye from one successful combination to the next. You're striving to create individual combinations that add interest and fend off the monotony of hosta, hosta, hosta. But you're also trying to create combos that contribute and connect to the overall landscape.

WHAT'S MY SHADE?

There are more shade-plant options these days than ever before, but you still have to pick those that work within the light levels prevalent in your garden. How do you do this? Monitor the hours of sunlight to pair the right plants successfully to your location. Some areas will likely get more light than others, and you may surprise yourself by finding that there are pockets of full sun and partial shade in your shade garden. Be honest with yourself when assessing your light levels. It is easy to make ourselves believe that we get that extra hour or two of sun to justify adding a sexy new plant to the garden. Even if the plant survives, it will not thrive if it doesn't receive its minimum light requirements—not very sexy.

When you have recorded your hours of shade, translate them into terms that you'll see when buying plants:

• **FULL SHADE:** Site receives less than 3 hours of sun per day.

• **PARTIAL SHADE:** Site receives 3 hours to 5 hours of sun per day.

• **FULL SUN:** Site receives more than 5 hours of sun per day.

1 'Aureola' Japanese forest grass (*Hakonechloa macra* 'Aureola', Zones 5–9)

2 'Red Ruffles' coleus (*Solenostemon scutellarioides* 'Red Ruffles', Zone 11)

3 'Frances Williams' hosta (*Hosta* 'Frances Williams', Zones 3–9)

A LITTLE COLOR GOES A LONG WAY

What's the first thing that comes to mind when you think of a shade garden? Probably not color. When color is used, however, a little bit can make an impact. In the combination shown in the photo above, 'Red Ruffles' coleus adds a splash of rich color that ties the combo to the warm, reddish tones of the stone path and a burgundy Japanese maple in the background. The large variegated leaves of 'Frances Williams' hosta create a focal point and complement the deep color of the coleus and the fine-textured foliage of 'Aureola' Japanese forest grass. Although hostas are often seen going solo in a shade garden, they look best when paired with other plants.

When you're adding color, don't think of the color in isolation. The color of the heuchera in the top photo on the facing page relates to the Japanese maple's canopy of foliage but, more important, creates depth and separation among the other plants. Just the right amount of variegated and chartreuse foliage can add further interest to an otherwise dark grouping. In the photo, three hosta

1. Emperor I® Japanese maple (*Acer palmatum* 'Wolff', Zones 5–8)

2. 'Aureola' Japanese forest grass (*Hakonechloa macra* 'Aureola', Zones 5–9)

3. 'Patriot' hosta (*Hosta* 'Patriot', Zones 3–9)

4. Japanese painted fern (*Athyrium niponicum* var. *pictum*, Zones 5–8)

5. 'Frances Williams' hosta (*Hosta* 'Frances Williams', Zones 3–9)

6. 'Obsidian' heuchera (*Heuchera* 'Obsidian', Zones 3–8)

7. 'Blue Angel' hosta (*Hosta* 'Blue Angel', Zones 3–9)

1. Korean wax bells (*Kirengeshoma palmata*, Zones 5–8)

2. Three-flower maple (*Acer triflorum*, Zones 5–7)

3. 'Frances Williams' hosta (*Hosta* 'Frances Williams', Zones 3–9)

4. 'Aureola' Japanese forest grass (*Hakonechloa macra* 'Aureola', Zones 5–9)

5. Accent® White impatiens (*Impatiens walleriana* Accent White, annual)

6. 'Jack Frost' brunnera (*Brunnera macrophylla* 'Jack Frost', Zones 3–7)

varieties are separated by contrasting plant textures and leaf colors, making each one special while also complementing their bed mates.

Annuals in a border not only boost the scene with continuous color but also help fill in gaps when perennial plantings aren't mature enough to do the work on their own. Impatiens is an easy annual to grow in shade, but also consider begonias (*Begonia* spp. and cvs., USDA Hardiness Zones 8–11), torenia (*Torenia* spp. and cvs., Zones 10–11), and foliage favorites such as coleus (*Solenostemon scutellarioides* cvs., Zone 11), hypoestes (*Hypoestes* spp. and cvs., Zones 10–11), and tradescantia (*Tradescantia* spp. and cvs., Zones 8–11)—all treated as annuals in Minnesota but as perennials in other regions. Add even more interest with details like the beautiful bark of three-flower maple.

1. Angelonia (*Angelonia angustifolia* cv., annual)
2. 'The Rocket' ligularia (*Ligularia stenocephala* 'The Rocket', Zones 4–8)
3. 'Lavender Mist' meadow rue (*Thalictrum rochebrunianum* 'Lavender Mist', Zones 5–9)
4. 'Aureola' Japanese forest grass (*Hakonechloa macra* 'Aureola', Zones 5–9)
5. 'Blue Angel' hosta (*Hosta* 'Blue Angel', Zones 3–9)
6. 'Nikko Blue' hydrangea (*Hydrangea macrophylla* 'Nikko Blue', Zones 6–9)

1. Accent White impatiens (*Impatiens walleriana* Accent White, annual)
2. 'Northern Pride' Siberian cypress (*Microbiota decussata* 'Northern Pride', Zones 3–7)
3. Bur oak (*Quercus macrocarpa*, Zones 3–9)
4. 'Love Pat' hosta (*Hosta* 'Love Pat', Zones 3–9)
5. 'Obsidian' heuchera (*Heuchera* 'Obsidian', Zones 3–8)
6. 'Sum and Substance' hosta (*Hosta* 'Sum and Substance', Zones 3–9)

EVEN IN SHADE, SCALE IS IMPORTANT

Sometimes you need a large group of herbaceous perennials to provide impact and appropriate scale, such as near the foundation of a home. Layering bands of contrasting textures, shapes, heights, and colors add depth, interest, and drama. You'll want something along the edge of a large grouping to highlight the edge while drawing the viewer's eye to other plants. The bright chartreuse foliage of Japanese forest grass works well. Include a group of tall plants to offer height and transparency without compromising the view from any windows behind them.

Trees, like pines, can be added to your garden plan to offer year-round stability as the flowers come and go throughout the seasons. But when you already have a lot of mature trees to contend with, you need to consider the size of the trees when selecting plants. For example, when you have massive oak trees, you need large masses of perennials to compete with them (see the photo at left). Big trees, however, are the bullies of the shade-garden

playground. They are the first in line to take the majority of water and nutrients, leaving little for the plants beneath them. Curb the effects of these bullies' bad habits by taking extra care to provide adequate water, fertility, and organic matter to your shade plants. With a little special attention, an under-the-tree garden holds up and blends right in with the rest of the landscape.

UNITE A DIVIDED SPACE WITH SIMILAR PLANTS

When your garden is split in half by a path, you need to unite the opposing sides. To ensure each side remains connected, repeat the same or similar plants. For example, in the photo above, Japanese painted fern, 'Aureola' Japanese forest grass, 'Nikko Blue' hydrangea, Emperor I Japanese maple, and 'Blue Angel' hosta are all duplicated on the opposite side of the path. Even small trees can be paired to enhance the connection. Japanese maples add

1. Japanese painted fern (*Athyrium niponicum* var. *pictum*, Zones 5–8)
2. 'Chidori Red' ornamental kale (*Brassica oleracea* 'Chidori Red', annual)
3. 'Frances Williams' hosta (*Hosta* 'Frances Williams', Zones 3–9)
4. 'Aureola' Japanese forest grass (*Hakonechloa macra* 'Aureola', Zones 5–9)
5. 'Blue Angel' hosta (*Hosta* 'Blue Angel', Zones 3–9)
6. Emperor I Japanese maple (*Acer palmatum* 'Wolff', Zones 5–8)
7. 'Nikko Blue' hydrangea (*Hydrangea macrophylla* 'Nikko Blue', Zones 6–9)
8. Angelonia (*Angelonia angustifolia* cv., annual)
9. 'Patriot' hosta (*Hosta* 'Patriot', Zones 3–9)
10. 'Chalet' Swiss stone pine (*Pinus cembra* 'Chalet', Zones 3–7)

essential color and can offer some transitional height between a canopy of mature oaks and lower herbaceous perennials and small shrubs. When your garden has a pocket or two of full sun, take advantage with a couple sun-loving pine trees. A pine is right at home alongside its shady neighbors.

Maintaining a beautiful border doesn't have to be a full-time job.

✓ **ECO-FRIENDLY OPTION**
✓ **HOW-TO**
✓ **LOW-MAINTENANCE IDEAS**
✓ **PLANT SUGGESTIONS**

HOW TO REDUCE
MAINTENANCE

When her huge garden became too much for garden expert Sydney Eddison, she realized it was time to make some changes. Using the time-saving tactics shared here can make your garden easier to care for too.

A FEW YEARS AGO, HAVING ARRIVED AT THE STARTLING AGE of 70, I realized that it might be a good idea to start replacing some of the perennials in the garden with less-demanding shrubs. At a leisurely pace and with the help of Brid Craddock, a talented gardener and designer who comes for half a day a week, I began making minor changes. Then a drastic and heartbreaking change was thrust upon me: My husband, Martin, died.

Although he was never a gardener, we had functioned as a team for 45 years. Martin mowed the lawn in the summer, vacuumed up the leaves in the fall, and made the power equipment purr with goodwill. After retiring, he took on the grocery shopping, errands, and a dozen other household tasks so that I could spend more time gardening and writing. In his absence, everything has suffered.

But to allow the garden—the living, ever-changing story of our lives—to go to wrack and ruin would have been unthinkable. So I have spent the past year trying to figure out what I can do to streamline operations and how to get help doing the things that are beyond me. So far, I am holding my own. Here are the simple but significant adaptations I've made to my gardening habits.

COVER YOUR BEDS WITH MULCH

My garden is large—perhaps an acre and a half—but simple, as befits a former cow pasture. A 100-ft.-long perennial border follows the contours of the east-facing hillside. Behind it, paths run athwart the slope in the shade of overhanging maples and among deciduous shrubs underplanted with ferns and hostas.

The lawn stretches north between the long border and a huge, old juniper hedge. The so-called "new borders," dug in 1990, partially enclose this panel of lawn. Beyond these beds lie shade plantings and the woodland garden. A crescent bed planted chiefly with daylilies is the most recent addition.

It has always been a trick, keeping up such a large place. But settling for tough, ordinary perennials—like daylilies (*Hemerocallis* cvs., USDA Hardiness Zones 3–10), rudbeckias (*Rudbeckia* spp. and cvs., Zones 3–11), sedums

ABOVE Tough perennials like Sedum work well in a low-maintenance garden.

LEFT Mulch makes sense. Three inches of hoarded, year-old leaves deter weed growth, conserve moisture, and provide food for plants as they break down.

Add woody plants where perennials reigned. Here, daylilies have been gradually replaced by shrubs that typically need pruning only once a year, as opposed to the deadheading and dividing required by many perennials.

(*Sedum* spp. and cvs., Zones 3–9), and catmints (*Nepeta* spp. and cvs., Zones 3–8)—worked well enough. And mulch solved what otherwise might have been a real maintenance problem.

Introduced to the benefits of organic mulch 25 years ago, I've been covering the perennial beds with year-old leaves ever since. This management technique has allowed me to garden, almost single-handedly, for a great many years. I gather leaves into an expansive pile in the fall. In spring, I mulch every square inch of soil between the perennials with 3 inches of these hoarded leaves. This layer of leaves shades out weed seedlings, conserves moisture, and breaks down during the season, providing organic plant food.

Shredded wood-chip mulch, purchased in bulk, is the next best thing. Brid and I have been using it in the wilder parts of the garden: along the paths, on the shrub plantings, under a pair of old apple trees, and on the crescent bed. It doesn't break down as quickly and is heavier than the leaf mulch. It also lasts longer and has proved the solution to managing these large, rough areas. These efforts should be all that is necessary for the season, except for occasional weed pulling.

REPLACE PERENNIALS WITH SHRUBS AND TREES

In the perennial beds, I have accelerated the replacement of perennials. Daylilies and false sunflowers (*Heliopsis helianthoides*, Zones 4–9) found new homes with friends and neighbors. In their place, I planted a dwarf Alberta spruce (*Picea glauca* var. *albertiana* 'Conica', Zones 2–6) and a narrow, compact arborvitae (*Thuja* cv., Zones 2–9). Happily, the evergreens have proved a great addition with their year-round color and solid, conical forms. In another area, a mass of asters has given way to the vase shape and bronze foliage of an eastern ninebark (*Physocarpus opulifolius* 'Diabolo', Zones 3–7).

Last fall, Brid and I embarked on an ambitious overhaul. Many daylilies were sacrificed to make way for a linden viburnum (*Viburnum dilatatum* 'Asian Beauty', Zones 5–8), a weigela (*Weigela florida* 'Variegata Nana', Zones 5–8), two compact oakleaf hydrangeas (*Hydrangea quercifolia* 'Sikes Dwarf', Zones 5–9), a golden spirea

PLANTS FOR TIDY EDGES

PLANT NAME	ZONES
FOR SUNNY SPOTS	
BLUE OAT GRASS (*Helictotrichon sempervirens*)	4–9
'BLUE WONDER' CATMINT (*Nepeta racemosa* 'Blue Wonder')	4–8
'HAMELN' FOUNTAIN GRASS (*Pennisetum alopecuroides* 'Hameln')	6–9
LESSER CATMINT (*Calamintha nepeta*)	5–9
SEDUMS (*Sedum* spp. and cvs.)	3–9
VARIEGATED LIRIOPE (*Liriope muscari* 'Variegata')	6–10
FOR SHADED AREAS	
BARRENWORTS (*Epimedium* spp. and cvs.)	5–9
BIGROOT GERANIUM (*Geranium macrorrhizum*)	4–8
GINGERS (*Asarum* spp. and cvs.)	2–9
HELLEBORES (*Helleborus* spp. and cvs.)	4–9
HOSTAS (*Hosta* spp. and cvs.)	3–9
VANCOUVERIA (*Vancouveria hexandra*)	5–8

Liriope

Hosta

Instead of digging in new border lines, use a string trimmer to keep the grass low and the edges manicured.

(*Spiraea japonica* 'Gold Mound', Zones 4–9), and a small but ravishing variegated Korean dogwood (*Cornus kousa* 'Gold Star', Zones 5–8). Most of these shrubs need pruning only once a year, instead of the regular deadheading, staking, and frequent division that many perennials require.

Perhaps the quickest route to lower maintenance in a flower bed is the elimination of plants that require even a little too much care. Gone from my garden are the balloon flowers and Russian sage; both have lax stems that invariably flop over. While I miss them, the beds are less trouble and look better. In the long run, a beautiful border is a manageable one. Fewer kinds of perennials, each with their own individual demands, make for ease of management.

SIMPLIFY YOUR APPROACH TO EDGES

Harder than giving up a bit of variety within the beds is letting go of their once immaculately cut edges. Edging every bed once or twice a season is just too time-consuming now. But I have learned to live with a reasonably tidy edge maintained using a string trimmer. The trick is to leave a space between the edge and the plants, to keep that space weeded, and to trim carefully and uniformly.

Another strategy that helps maintain the lines of the beds is to choose foreground plants that remain neat and attractive all season. In the sun, I favor low-growing grasses and naturally compact, orderly perennials that have good-looking foliage and either bloom for a long time or recover quickly from shearing.

DON'T RUSH TO FILL SPACES

For the disciplined gardener, an easy way to reduce maintenance is to resist filling every gap that appears in the landscape. I am not a disciplined gardener, but adopting a wait-and-see attitude toward empty spaces has paid dividends. For 15 years, a lovely flowering cherry (*Prunus* 'Hally Jolivette', Zones 6–8) flourished among the dwarf conifers in my island bed. Then, quite suddenly, it died.

With uncharacteristic restraint, I did not replace the tree, and I was glad because the conifers rejoiced to find themselves in full sun once again. The 'Blue Star' juniper (*Juniperus squamata* 'Blue Star', Zones 4–9) became bluer, and the golden false cypress (*Chamaecyparis pisifera* 'Filifera Aurea Nana', Zones 4–8), which had remained green in the shade of the cherry, was restored to its former bright self. Then, a couple of years later, voles set upon the juniper, leaving only the Alberta spruce and the false cypress. In terms of design and balance, that was all right, too; the remaining shrubs needed the extra room. The garden changes, and the plants adapt. The gardener must do the same.

Gardening is all about change, about hanging on and letting go. At a certain stage, the gardener must look at every plant and ask hard questions: "Have I the time and energy to give this plant what it needs? And if not, do I love it enough to give it what it needs anyway?"

Often, alas, the answer may be no. But then there are the exceptions, like a blue-and-white-striped balloon flower. It was given to me by a perfect stranger. He found it as a seedling in his aunt's garden and named it "Louise" in her honor. I could never willingly part with Louise. In some ways, I just can't let go.

Adapt to garden changes. Instead of replacing a flowering cherry (top) when it died, the adjacent plants were allowed to fill in (above).

✓ **HOW-TO**
✓ **LOW-MAINTENANCE IDEAS**
✓ **LANDSCAPE SOLUTIONS**

❁

PERFECT EDGES

Designing crisp, clean garden lines is easy; simply follow the four steps gardener Ray Baker has devised to keep your lawn and flower beds looking neat.

AS AN INTERIOR DESIGNER, I'VE ALWAYS KNOWN THE IMPORTANCE of well-defined lines. Inside the house or out, a clean, smooth line provides a finished look and a sense of clarity to an area. In my garden, a razor-sharp edge serves as a stage that sets off the careful planning and maintenance I do. Such meticulous attention to detail doesn't require a lot of work.

I use four simple steps to create and freshen up my edges in spring, giving my beds the crisp lines that reflect the effort I put into my garden. By creating or re-creating an edge, removing turf, honing the edge, and mulching the bed I am able to showcase the beauty of the garden. Clean edges are a wonderful way to add polish to any yard.

Clean, neat edges make a garden look well maintained.

An edger makes clean lines quickly.

Hand tools cut through grass well but don't make neat curves.

CREATE (OR RE-CREATE) AN EDGE

The first step is to cut the edge. If you are creating a new bed, you'll need to use a garden hose to mark your desired lines. If you are freshening up an existing bed, you can jump right in.

The traditional way to do this is to use either a spade or a half-moon edger to move along the line you've set out. Neither tool does a great job of cutting curves, and it can be difficult to evaluate the course you're taking as you move along.

I use an Edge Hog® from Black & Decker®, a tool with a circular blade on wheels. I simply walk behind the tool as it rolls easily along, cutting a continuous 1½-inch-deep line into the soil. The wheels give the tool the mobility to make nice curves, and you can clearly see as you cut, making it easy to evaluate and revise the line of your bed. The edger simplifies the daunting task of caring for my 4-acre garden, with its 5,000 linear feet of edging.

REMOVE THE TURF

Once you've established your edge, refine it with a spade, deepening the cut to 4 inches to 6 inches. If you are cutting a new bed, you also need to cut the turf on the inside of the bed with the spade. The loosened turf can then be removed easily by hand. The goal is to create an edge at a 90-degree angle to the turf.

LEFT Once you've cut through the grass pull it out by hand.

BELOW For an extra-clean look trim with shears after removing the clumps of grass.

ABOVE Add mulch to the finished bed.

HONE THE EDGE

I like my edges to be razor sharp, so I place hand shears vertically along the trench wall and cut any remaining grass blades from the edge. Hold the shears carefully to avoid destroying the right angle of the edge. I repeat this step two or three times during the growing season to keep my edges looking groomed.

MULCH THE BED

The final step is to put down 2 inches to 3 inches of mulch on the bed. The mulch not only suppresses weeds but also adds a rich, dark color to the edge. I mulch right up to the edge of the turf to create a gentle slope from the bottom of the edge to the top of the bed (see the drawing at right).

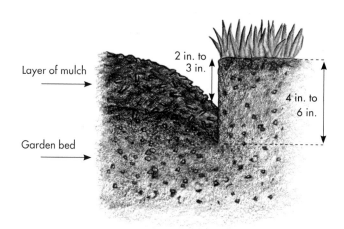

Layer of mulch

2 in. to 3 in.

4 in. to 6 in.

Garden bed

FOUR WAYS TO
REMOVE SOD

Removing grass to make way for a new flower bed can be intimidating, but it needn't be. Plant ecologist Steve Carroll suggests a variety of the methods so that you can find the one that suits you best.

IF YOU ARE THINKING ABOUT TURNING AN AREA OF LAWN INTO a garden bed, your first step will be to get rid of the grass. You can take different routes to accomplish this: Those that yield quick results can require considerable effort, while less labor-intensive methods may take at least a season to produce results.

Four techniques—digging, tilling, smothering, and using herbicides—can turn well-established turf into a bed ready for planting. Each method has its pros and cons, but all will get you one step closer to the bed you've been dreaming of.

Digging by hand is the simplest approach to removing grass.

DIG

Digging produces quick, clean results and allows you to plant your garden immediately. But using a spade or fork to remove sod can result in a lot of sweat and sore muscles. If the sod is in good condition, you can use it elsewhere in your yard.

If you'd like to reuse your sod, water the area to make the soil easier to work. The soil should be moist but not soggy. Saturated soil is not only heavy but also susceptible to compaction, which leads to poor plant growth.

Using an edger or sharp spade cut the sod into parallel strips 1 foot wide. These strips can then be cut into 1-foot to 2-foot lengths, depending on the density of the turf and the thickness of the pieces. Next, pry up one end of a piece of sod and slide the spade or fork under it. Cut through any deep taproots, and lift out the precut piece, making sure to include the grass's fibrous roots. If the underside of the sod contains much loose soil, a fork may work best, as this soil can be shaken back onto the surface when the sod is lifted.

If you skip the crosscut step, roll up the strips and keep peeling the strip back. Keep in mind, though, that these rolls will be heavy. If you are installing a large bed, consider renting a sod cutter. These steel-bladed, plowlike tools are more efficient than spades for large jobs, and they come in human- and gas-powered models.

Inspect your new bed's subsoil (and the underside of the sod if it will be reused). Once the sod is gone, look for and destroy potential pests, such as the larvae of May/June beetles. Remove any rocks, remaining clumps of grass, and sizable roots.

One drawback to sod removal is the significant loss of organic material, which greatly contributes to the health of plants. It must be restored as compost, as aged manure, or in some other form. Usually, topsoil must also be replaced. Some of it may be shaken out of the sod that was removed, but you will probably need more, especially if you need to raise the level of the bed.

TILL

Breaking up sod with a tiller requires some muscle, but most of the work is done by the tiller's engine. Small tillers can usually handle previously worked gardens, but breaking up well-established sod requires a heavier, rear-tine unit and may require more than one pass. Large tillers can be hard to maneuver. You will likely need to carve the edge of your new bed with a spade or edger, especially if the border is curved. After tilling the bed, remove and shake the soil from any remaining clumps of grass.

One advantage of tilling is that the original organic matter is retained in the garden as the sod is turned under. You can add organic matter by forking or shoveling compost, manure, grass clippings, or leaf mold onto the sod before tilling.

A tilled bed can be planted immediately, but the process brings to the surface weed seeds that may germinate and cause problems later. You may also wind up inadvertently propagating some weeds like quack grass, which can send up new shoots from the small pieces of its chopped-up rhizome. Canada thistle does the same thing with its severed lateral roots. If you keep the soil moist and delay planting by a couple of weeks, you can pull, hoe, or otherwise dispatch these weeds as they emerge.

SMOTHER

Perhaps the easiest way to eliminate grass is to smother it using plastic, newspaper, or cardboard. Depending on the time of year and material used, this can take several months.

If you are using plastic, stretch a light-excluding type over the lawn. With the edges securely anchored, the temperature under the plastic will increase dramatically. The high temperatures and lack of light will eventually kill the grass, although they can also destroy beneficial organisms. Plastic can be covered for aesthetic purposes, but it isn't biodegradable and should eventually be

Several layers of newspaper will block light, causing the grass to die. A few months later, the soil is ready for planting.

removed. If you cover the grass during the summer, you can plant by the following spring

Laying cardboard or newspaper over the grass is a better alternative. Cover these biodegradable materials with grass clippings, leaf mold, mulch, or compost to hold the layers in place, keep in moisture, and add organic matter (see the photo on the facing page). Lay down six to eight sheets of newspaper; use paper printed with black-and-white ink only, as colored ink may contain heavy metals. Wet the newspaper to help keep it in place. Newspaper and cardboard do not increase temperature as much as plastic, but they eliminate light, causing chlorophyll to break down. Once this happens, photosynthesis stops and the smothered plants die. To plant right away, just plug mature plants into holes that you have punched through the paper to the underlying soil.

APPLY HERBICIDES

I favor the other three methods over using herbicides, perhaps because I can immediately see any damage I cause (slicing through an earthworm with a spade, for example). Too often in our dealings with nature, unanticipated effects of chemical use have been discovered only years later. The herbicide option may be reasonable if you have appropriate equipment and follow safety instructions and application recommendations carefully.

LEFT Herbicides kill grass quickly, but it's often unclear what else they do in the soil.

THE PROS & CONS

DIG

PROS: Permits immediate planting; avoids use of chemicals and loud power tools

CONS: Is labor intensive; exposes subsoil to weed seeds by eliminating vegetative cover; removes organic matter

TILL

PROS: Retains organic matter; is quicker and easier than digging; permits immediate planting

CONS: Is difficult on rocky sites and in wet or clay soils; turns up weed seeds; propagates certain weeds

SMOTHER

PROS: Does not require the physical effort of removing or turning under sod; leaves original organic matter in place; does not disrupt soil structure

CONS: Delays planting up to several months; may kill beneficial organisms if using plastic

APPLY HERBICIDES

PROS: Is relatively simple and quick for gardeners experienced in herbicide use; makes it easier to remove or turn grass

CONS: Risks injuring or killing nearby plants; can result in environmental contamination, personal injury, or harm to beneficial organisms when used improperly

A pile planted with daylilies and irises settled into a handsome bed within a few seasons.

✓ ECO-FRIENDLY OPTION
✓ HOW-TO
✓ LOW-MAINTENANCE IDEAS

❁

BUILD A BED
WITHOUT BREAKING YOUR BACK

After moving to a larger property, Barbara Ashmun, a garden designer and frequent Fine Gardening *contributor, traded in the time-consuming and back-breaking work of digging beds, and instead devised this easy, earth-friendly, and people-friendly recipe for new planting spots.*

I'VE BUILT NEW BEDS TWO DIFFERENT WAYS: THE HARD WAY AND the easy way. When I did things the hard way, I'd slice the existing sod with an edger, dig up the strips with a spade, and stack them upside down to compost. Then, I'd dig about a foot down into the new bed, turn the soil over, break it into small chunks, add finished compost, turn it again, and mix compost and soil to make a uniform blend. Finally, I'd rake it all smooth and level, admiring the fine, crumbly texture. This was good exercise and satisfying work.

When I moved to a larger lot encompassing two-thirds of an acre, the very idea of improving so much dense, clay soil seemed overwhelming. I tried numerous bed-building experiments, but no matter how much tilling or amending I did, it was never enough. Hand-digging might have worked, but the Herculean effort required to spade my large garden from end to end made the task simply unimaginable.

So I began searching for easier ways to build new beds. Finally, I found one. It doesn't require much digging, I don't have to strip

SELECTING A SITE THAT WORKS

I think of my garden as a laboratory, a place to experiment with color, texture, and fragrance. It's already full of colorful beds where I arrange perennials and flowering shrubs into pleasing compositions. But I'm still experimenting, and before I embark on a new venture, I've got to prepare a new workshop.

Before looking for a new spot, I consider the needs of the plants I want to use. If I'm planning a home for shade-loving astilbes and hydrangeas, for example, I'll need to find bed space beneath the canopy of deciduous trees, or on the north side of the house.

Once I know my plants will be happy, I stroll around the yard, looking at potential places from different angles. Sometimes I sit on a garden bench or plop down on the lawn to study the scene. I might check out the views from inside the house, too. At this stage, I'm just playing with geometry, looking for a likely place to plunk down a new square, rectangle, circle, or oval bed.

This is also a good time to think about the eventual size of the future site's plants. When full grown, will they block a view or create one? If the new site is in front of a homely fence or shed, filling the bed with tall flowering shrubs and towering perennials will create a colorful screen.

Once I do get an idea for a bed, I use a garden hose (or two, if I'm thinking big) to outline the shape I've envisioned (see top left photo on the facing page). I aim for gracefully contoured beds that are in proportion with nearby planting areas. I think repeating shapes and sizes adds order and unity to larger designs.

One of the most common mistakes people make when preparing a new bed is skimping on its size. So, if you're wondering how big to make a new bed, remember that too big is almost always better than too small.

off the turf, and it costs almost nothing. In essence, I build a compost pile and let it ripen into a rich, organic bed that my plants just love. The process does take a little time, but if gardening has taught me anything, it's the joy of participating in the miracle of transformation. Turning seeds into flowers or leaves into soil makes me feel almost like an alchemist.

Now I build new beds whenever the inspiration strikes, but there's no question that fall is the ideal time to tackle the task. Autumn days are usually mild enough to make vigorous activity enjoyable. Materials for composting are plentiful: fallen leaves, spent flower foliage, and lawn clippings are everywhere. Perhaps best of all, in my mild climate, the compost cooks all winter, and by spring, when I'm anxious to get back into the garden, the bed is ready.

Fallen leaves, grass clippings, and sawdust are some of the ingredients used for on-site composting.

DON'T TEAR UP THE LAWN

I first learned there was a better, or at least an easier, bed-building technique in *The Ruth Stout No-Work Garden Book*. I'd also heard about it from friends. They all said the easy way to create good soil is to simply compost right on the site of your future bed. After putting the technique to the test several times, I've learned that it works. And along the way, I've added a few refinements of my own to make the process even easier.

The first step is defining the area that you're going to turn into a bed. I use a garden hose to outline the area (see the left photo above). I usually warm up the hose in the sun so it's soft and easy to work with. Heat makes it pliable enough to coax into whatever shape I've envisioned.

Once I decide on the shape and placement of the new bed, I use an edger and a shovel to dig a 6-inch-deep trench between the bed and the lawn (see the top right photo above). The trench keeps the edge crisp and stops the lawn from invading the bed.

Not that I worry too much about the lawn. In fact, I don't even bother to tear up the grass. Some folks spread newspaper, or even cardboard, on the turf to smother it. I've done that but find it unnecessary—the 3-foot-high piles of organic material I heap on the site kill the grass just as effectively (see the bottom photo at right). Once the new bed is planted with shrubs, perennials, or annuals, the roots of the new plants don't seem to have any problem growing through a layer of what was once turf.

BUILD THE BED

The key to the easy bed-building method is building a pile that is at least 3 feet high, so you need to have plenty of materials to compost. I heap on layers of grass clippings, leaves, spent rabbit litter, sawdust, vegetable peelings, half-finished compost from my bins, and old potting soil from last year's annual containers.

COLLECT COMPOST To get a hefty pile, you might think about networking with people in your neighborhood who are throwing out materials that would fuel a good compost pile. I've trained my neighbors to bring me tarploads of leaves after they've raked and wheelbarrows of grass clippings after they've mown. Landscapers who work in the neighborhood are glad to deliver pickup loads of grass clippings—they save a dump fee. They drop them onto a gigantic tarp that I lay out in the driveway, and I wheelbarrow the clippings to the new bed site. I also collect sawdust from a nearby woodworking shop, and straw bedding and manure from friends who have rabbits, chickens, or other animals. Loading the wheelbarrow with my bounty and maneuvering it back and forth from driveway to bed entails a fair amount of work, but to me it's easier than digging.

FINISH IT OFF Once the pile is in place, I finish it off by raking the materials into a soft, rounded mound (see the photo on the facing page). Then I sometimes even collect extra earthworms that wriggle out of the ground and onto the sidewalk after a rainstorm. I take them to the new bed site to help break down all the raw ingredients. "Get to work!" I tell the worms, and then dream of them busily burrowing, making rich, black soil while I relax and wait for spring to arrive.

IN COLDER CLIMATES If you live where it's cold, and winter puts the local landscape into a deep freeze, a new bed prepared in fall may not be ready by spring. You could speed the process along by adding an accelerant to the pile. (You can find accelerants for compost-making at most hardware stores or garden centers.) Another option would be draping a sheet of black plastic over the pile to absorb sunlight and keep it warm. Some gardeners say white or clear plastic works just as well. Be sure to punch holes into the plastic so water and air can get into the pile.

In the meantime, you'll have to cope with one of the easy method's biggest drawbacks: It's ugly. You'll have to spend several months looking at an oversized heap of decomposing stuff that looks like a pile of dirt.

LEFT For a finishing touch, use a spade to clean and neaten the border and keep the lawn out of the planting area.

FACING PAGE Instead of digging down, build a compost pile on top of the site for a new bed. Once it's ready, rake the raw materials into a mound and let them compost for a season or two.

LET NATURE TAKE OVER

When I've finished building the pile, I relax and let nature take its course. Insects and microorganisms will dine on this fabulous feast and transform it into crumbly soil over the next six months.

If I'm in a big hurry, I turn the pile often and keep it damp. If I'm in a bigger hurry, I buy finished compost, pile it up 3 feet high in the shape of the bed, and plant. I did that one fall, and thought I would be struck by lightning for sheer decadence, but instead I enjoyed a beautiful island bed of Siberian irises and daylilies the following spring (see the photo on p. 56).

Would I go back to the hard way of bed building? I figure I have three choices: I can spend energy to hand dig and amend soil, spend money to buy finished compost to pile on, or spend time waiting for raw materials to break down. At this point, I like the last option best. I'm willing to wait. There's plenty of gardening to do in other borders while the compost cooks. And it's fun to participate in a natural process, creating a small ecosystem in which the slow process of decomposition gets an assist from soft rains, warm sunshine, and wriggling worms. I love being a small part of a much bigger scheme.

Dig out and discard the plants you don't want. After removing the existing plants, rebuild the bed with a new vision in mind.

REMAKE A BED

Fine Gardening *contributor Linda Wesley's design style and plant tastes changed, she realized her garden needed a complete overhaul. So she dug in and dug up, and created a more naturalistic garden.*

EARLY ON, WHEN I BEGAN LEARNING ABOUT GARDENING, I went to a garden club lecture given by local gardening legend Sydney Eddison. I sat at a table surrounded by matronly club members who asked me what I specialized in. I told them quite naively that I loved all flowers, that I hadn't yet found one I didn't like. With eyebrows raised and coy smiles covered politely by their napkins, the ladies said, "That's nice, dear."

But it was true, and as the years went by my garden grew with one of this and one of that, or with impetuous desires to have certain plants completely unsuited to our land (like heavenly scented roses, for example). In the end, my whimsical approach became my garden's undoing. Every year by midsummer, it was a floppy mess, a hodgepodge that was neither pleasing nor promising of better things to come. I wish the garden club ladies had clued me in way back when, but then I probably wouldn't have listened.

Right about this same time, I fell under the influence of a new gardening aesthetic, that of a more naturalistic approach to design. Thanks to the words and work of a number of insightful individuals like Rick Darke, Piet Oudolf, and James van Sweden and Wolfgang Oehme, I became more interested in plants like

LEFT Create a staging area. Carefully remove and divide the plants you wish to reuse, setting them aside on a tarp in the shade and taking special care to keep their roots moist.

RIGHT Now is the time to amend the soil. A garden renovation offers the perfect opportunity to add soil amendments like peat moss and aged manure to the beds before replanting.

grasses that glimmer in the late-day light and native perennials that are as tough as nails. And I found myself leaning toward a design sense that relied on bold groupings of plants and on foliage and texture as much as flowers. So, early in spring, I decided to take on a major overhaul of two large garden beds.

TIME FOR A CHANGE

I planned to start with a clean slate, by first digging up and temporarily holding most of the plants that were in the beds, then replanting with a new design that incorporated the old with the new. I resolved to remove the plants that were floundering (the roses that didn't get enough sun and the daylilies the deer love), divide and rejuvenate the ones that were thriving, like catmints *Nepeta* spp.), bee balms (*Monarda* cvs.), and irises (*Iris siberica* and *I. virginica*), and get out my checkbook for a big plant order. I purchased some of the new plants

through a landscaper friend who got me a good price on potted plants in quantity, some came as gifts from gardening friends, and others were ordered from a bare-root perennial nursery with a wide selection of grasses and natives—just the plants I was looking for.

DO THE OVERHAUL JUST BEFORE IT RAINS

Early spring is the best time to dig up and temporarily hold plants because they don't have a lot of foliage, and the cool temperatures and steady rains of spring help sustain them. By early April, I had sent in my mail order, and I began acquiring potted plants from my landscaping connection.

Toward the end of the month, the nursery sent me a card saying my order would arrive in a few days, and at that point I started to empty out the beds. I transplanted some plants to different parts of the garden and set up a holding area for the rest. I spread out a large tarp in the shade and began lifting the remaining perennials. I set them all on the tarp and gave their roots a gentle soaking. Most perennials can tolerate being out of the ground for a few days, as long as you keep their roots moist and set them out of harsh sunlight.

Once the beds were empty, I amended the soil with cow manure and peat moss, which I worked in with a metal garden rake. The weather forecast was calling for an extended period of light rain—perfect for planting. With

Prepare bare root plants for planting by soaking the roots in water for several hours to remoisten them after their long journey. Trim away any damaged roots or leaves.

the groundwork done, my stage was set, and it seemed that even Mother Nature would cooperate. I waited for the plants to arrive.

GET PLANTS IN THE GROUND PROMPTLY

The UPS man left two good-size boxes on my doorstep that Friday. I unpacked them and inspected the shipment. Just before planting the following day, I soaked the roots for several hours. If you can't plant them right away, it's OK to store the plants in a cool, dry spot for a few days, but no more.

I'd worked out a rough design based on all the plants assembled so I could keep track of what I wanted to go where. So, as it started to drizzle on Saturday morning, I began to plant, starting at the back of the beds and working my way forward. I'd planned for large clumps of individual species, grouping three or five or more together. No more one of this and one of that, except for a few large perennials like *Ligularia* species that could hold their own alone.

As I finished an area, I watered the plants thoroughly. I modified the design somewhat as I planted. A drawing on paper can't portray the real, three-dimensional conditions of a garden, so in any planting scheme, be prepared to be flexible and make changes as you go. At the end of two days, both large beds were planted.

The following weekend, I mulched the beds with some cedar bark mulch. And as the season progressed, I made sure the plantings were well watered during dry spells. It's vital to provide extra water if needed for new plants their first season in the ground, while they're putting down roots and becoming established. And it's also wise not to

expect too much too soon, as plants need time to mature. I knew it would be a couple of years before these beds would look their best.

It has been three years now since the overhaul, and I'm pleased with the results. I hate to admit how many failures occurred, but hey, that gave me an opportunity to try more new plants. I've added more native perennials, and I fill in gaps each spring with annuals. The grasses have grown big and tall and lovely, and now the garden looks good from early spring to autumn, and even into winter. Some plants don't seem completely happy, though, so they may come out this year. A garden is always evolving —that's the fun of it for me.

BEFORE

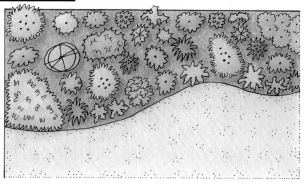

AFTER

The author's border had evolved in a way she no longer found appealing, so she pulled out the hodgepodge of plants that was there and replaced them with more naturalistic drifts of plants suited to the site.

Cover woody shrubs with burlap in winter to protect them from hungry animals.

❋

PUT YOUR
GARDEN TO BED

Like most chores, you might want to avoid end-of-the-year garden cleanup, but don't give in to the impulse. By performing a few simple tasks, you can wrap up the season on a high note. Just follow horticulture expert Jennifer Benner's easy tips.

AS MUCH AS I LOVE GARDENING, I MUST ADMIT THAT I LOOK forward to putting my garden to bed at the end of the season. In the same way my plants need a rest, I like my own dormancy period, which allows me the time to get cozy, hunker down, and neglect my unrealistic winter to-do list. When spring arrives, I will kick myself for not having picked up the book I meant to read, painted the guest bedroom, or finished the scarf that will now have to be next year's Christmas present to my sister. But the one thing I won't regret is the time I took in the fall to ready my garden for winter and to get a jump-start on spring chores.

My gardening efforts in autumn range from reassessing the design of my beds to cleaning and storing pots. I also protect my vulnerable plants so that I am less likely to have to replace them after winter's wrath has passed. This proactive approach works well for me because I garden on the go during the hectic spring and summer months. Here are some things I do to get ready for the following year.

In the fall, ready the plants for a spring move by root pruning.

plant to generate new roots inside the circle. These roots will give the plant a head start when it's moved to its new location and help it get established quickly.

TIDY BEDS AND CONTAINERS

I also concentrate my fall-cleaning efforts on my perennial beds and borders. After a couple of hard frosts, I cut back my perennials to a height of 3 inches to 6 inches using a pair of hand pruners or, sometimes, a string trimmer. This task not only saves time in spring but also keeps harmful insects and pathogens from finding a cozy place to spend the winter. I spare plants like ornamental grasses, purple coneflowers, and black-eyed Susans because they provide food for wildlife and winter interest for me. Because some plants don't like being cut back completely (and I can never remember which ones they are), I don't cut my perennials all the way to the ground until spring. The remaining stubs serve as reminders of where plants are. I deposit the debris into my compost pile, which generates temperatures high enough to kill any pests and pathogens that may be present.

To be on the safe side, any plants infested with a pest or disease—or those prone to such afflictions—do not go into my compost pile. The dead leaves of plants like hostas, for example, can harbor fugitive slugs and snails, while plants like bee balm and garden phlox are often plagued with powdery mildew. The debris from these plants goes straight into the trash to prevent the problems from being reintroduced to my garden.

If I have time, I will rake out my shrub beds, but I don't stress if it doesn't get done. Woody plants don't seem to be as susceptible as perennials to the insects and diseases that live in the debris, and the leaves provide a layer of insulation against winter.

Having a compulsive desire to keep everything neat and organized, I can never call it the end of the gardening season without cleaning up my containers. If they are not bound for the basement to overwinter a treasured tender plant, I dump their contents into the compost pile and sanitize my pots before storing them for the winter. This practice helps prevent any pests or diseases from setting up shop in next year's plantings. In spring, I just reach for a clean pot when I'm ready to plant.

DIVIDE AND TRANSPLANT

For me, the best time to plant, divide, and transplant is in early fall, when my garden layout is fresh in my mind and I can see the holes in my design. It's also a good time to get reacquainted with my plants and see which ones are dead, which are overgrown, and which need a better spot to succeed. Dividing overgrown perennials provides me with plants to solve design flaws and rejuvenates the parent plants at the same time. Planting and dividing in fall also gives my plants a season to become established, and they reward my efforts with better spring performance. I welcome plants to their new locations by turning a good amount of compost into their planting hole, giving them a light topdressing of a naturally derived fertilizer, and watering them thoroughly.

If I run out of time to transplant any woody plants in the fall, I plunge my spade into the soil around the base of the plant in a circle as if I were going to dig it up (see the photo above). This technique, called root pruning, makes it easier to dig up the plant in spring and encourages the

Protect young trees with tree wrap.

COVER NEW ADDITIONS WITH A BLANKET OF MULCH

Before my garden drifts off into its winter slumber, I provide some protection for vulnerable plants. Newly planted trees and shrubs get a 3-inch-deep layer of mulch to retain moisture and protect the soil from temperature fluctuations that cause frost heaving, which can expose crowns and roots to harsh winter weather. For my newly planted or shallow-rooted perennials, I wait until at least three hard freezes—when perennials are dormant—and insulate them by covering their crowns with a 2-inch-deep layer of dry leaves. An evergreen bough held in place with an 8-inch- or 10-inch-long anchoring pin or a rock placed on top keeps everything secure. The mulch prevents frost heaving and premature bud break. If I put the leaf mulch on before the plant is dormant, I might smother the plant or encourage disease to develop.

PREVENT DIEBACK AMONG EVERGREENS

Evergreens, especially those that are newly planted or exposed to wind, are vulnerable in winter because they still need to take in moisture. When the ground freezes, a lack of water can cause many leaves or even entire branches to dry up and die. To prevent this winter dieback, I spray an antidesiccant on the leaves. Antidesiccants (or antitranspirants) coat the leaves and slow down water loss from the plant. Over several months, the coating breaks down into microscopic powder that is blown away by wind or washed off by rain. I buy antidesiccants in concentrated form so that I can mix them in my spray tank. This yields a spray that is more even than what handheld, premixed bottles provide. Plus, if you have several plants to spray, the concentrate is more cost effective. It's best to apply these products on a late fall day when the temperatures haven't yet dropped below freezing and when wind won't hinder the accuracy of your aim.

To clean my containers, I first remove any remaining soil with a dry scrub brush. I then scour the pot inside and out with a solution of 10 parts water to 1 part bleach. Once the pots have dried, I stack them with newspaper or brown paper bags between them so that they don't stick together or break when moved. If I run out of time to clean my pots, I make sure to store them where they will be protected from harsh winter conditions.

WRAP YOUNG TREES TO PREVENT SUNSCALD

Young trees (those with trunks less than 4 inches in diameter) are prone to sunscald, or cracking caused by warm sun on a cold day. To prevent sunscald, I protect the trunks of young trees with tree wrap. The 4-inch-wide paper strip stands up to water but doesn't retain moisture, which can induce disease. Starting at the bottom and working my way up, I circle the trunk, slightly overlapping the wrap at each pass. Once I reach the top of the trunk, where the tree's branches begin, I secure the paper by wrapping it back around itself or tying it off. I remove the wrap when temperatures stop fluctuating severely in early spring. The wrap also protects the tree's bark from deer or rodent damage.

2

BEDS

SIMPLE FIXES
CAN MAKE A BIG DIFFERENCE

California landscape designer Genevieve Schmidt reveals how to make lackluster beds beautiful by sharing the four elements that many well-designed gardens have in common.

HAVE YOU ALWAYS WONDERED WHAT MAKES A GARDEN TRULY stunning? Sometimes the solution is simple: Spread some mulch, pull some weeds, or add some interesting plants. But other times, these minor adjustments don't do the trick. Over the years, I've noticed that successful garden beds have a lot in common: neat edges, bold focal points that direct the eye, beds that are in scale with their surroundings, and plants that are the appropriate size. If your beds seem to be missing that "wow" factor, it's possible that they are lacking one of these four things. So what should you do? Diagnose the problem, commit to solving it, and invest in making the correction. Yes, these fixes are labor intensive, but they will ultimately give you the garden you've always dreamed of. Here's how to start.

AFTER

Manufactured landscape edging makes borders and beds look neat, without routine maintenance.

BEFORE

The bed wrapping around this house lacked definition but improved when edged.

PERMANENTLY DEFINE THE EDGES

When lawn creeps into garden beds, it causes a wavy, messy line that's hard to keep neat. Until you install permanent edging, the grass and weeds will continue to creep in. Manufactured landscape edging saves you time and maintenance (because you have to install it only once) and is one of the easiest ways to make your garden look well kept. Even if you haven't weeded lately, a defined border can fool the eye into seeing the bed as tidier than it actually is.

There are three main options for permanent edging. Bender board is my favorite because it is the least noticeable (see the photo on p. 72). Brick and stone are pricey, but they can be installed in a weekend. Concrete curbing is the most expensive because it is usually installed by a licensed contractor.

Before installing your edging of choice, use a mattock or spade to cut a trench along the edge of your bed, clearing away the sod and weeds as you go. Be sure your edging rests about 1½ inches above soil level so that the edging will stop the rogue weeds and grass from "jumping the fence" into your beds. After installation, backfill with soil to secure the edging.

BEFORE

BEFORE Without a strong focal point, attention is drawn away from the plant and is instead placed on the background.

AFTER Attention-grabbing elements put the focus back on the bed.

AFTER

MAKE THE GARDEN
THE FOCUS

A garden should always have focal points that draw the eye toward standout plants or interesting objects while diverting attention away from the more functional areas of a property, like the side of a house. If a garden lacks any attention-grabbing elements, you tend to notice the background, which may be unattractive, and not the bed. This is a big problem if the poorly designed bed is located in a prominent area of the landscape.

CHOOSE THE FOCUS

Small trees or interesting shrubs make ideal focal points because they can grow large enough to make a bold statement and redirect attention away from large eyesores. In established beds, however, using a tree as a focal point usually means having to remove smaller plants to make room. If you don't want to remove anything, you can, instead, add objects, such as garden-art pieces, a water feature, some pottery, or a birdbath; these can be nestled in among what's already there. Although a focal point is often the largest element in a garden bed, it doesn't have to be; it just has to be interesting.

DETERMINE WHERE IT FITS BEST

When choosing a location for a focal point, the first thing to consider is from what vantage point you actually view your garden. Do you look out the window while doing dishes or is there a comfy chair on your patio that you like to sit in? Stand in those spots, and let your eyes wander; if an area is all right but isn't drawing attention, considering placing a focal point there.

UPSIZE YOUR BED

One of the most common mistakes gardeners make is underestimating how large a garden bed should be. A garden bed looks best when its depth is about one-third the height of the nearest and tallest visual element (such as a tree or your house). Applying this rule of thirds ensures that your garden beds are in scale with their surroundings and helps your home and landscape fit together visually.

If your garden bed is overflowing with living treasures, widening it can ease the maintenance needed to keep these plants in check. Also, if your garden appears too flattened out (see top photo below), you may need to widen the bed to get enough room to place a focal-point plant that is large enough to complement the strong lines of your home.

Start by visually estimating the height of the nearest tall element. For a foundation planting, this is most likely the roof of your house. If the roof peak is, for example, 21 feet tall, then, using the rule of thirds, you should increase the size of the bed to 7 feet deep. Remove any lawn inside the new border, and add compost to give the soil a boost. Once your bed is prepared, you can move around existing plants and add new ones to fill in the wider shape. The best time to resize a garden bed is in fall, when your plants are going into dormancy.

BEFORE

AFTER

BEFORE Small plants make the bed look flat.

AFTER Widening the bed and adding focal point plants complements the lines of the house.

HOW TO TAKE YOUR GARDEN BACK

A common issue in established gardens is the existence of problem plants: perennials that a gardener intentionally plants but that soon begin taking over a bed, making it look messy. In the bed shown below, a black-eyed Susan (*Rudbeckia* cv., Zones 3–9) is overstepping its bounds. Here's how to get things back in check.

IDENTIFY THE CAUSE, AND REMOVE THE OFFENDER

Whether your garden thug is reseeding or spreading underground, the first step in getting rid of it is to figure out what the roots look like. Gently dig around the periphery of the offending plant with a soil knife or trowel, and take note of the thickness and color of the roots. Once you know what to look for, follow each series of roots as far as it goes and remove every bit you can find, taking special care not to disturb the roots of the well-behaved plants nearby.

KEEP IT FROM COMING BACK

When you've removed as much of the rogue plant as you can, the next step is to prevent it from coming back. Chances are, you won't be able to remove every bit of the roots. Cardboard is an excellent solution for keeping problem plants from returning because it prevents both seeds and roots from sprouting. Place a layer of dampened cardboard on top of the soil (in the areas where you removed the plant), and cover it with a 3-inch- to 4-inch-deep layer of compost to keep it in place. You can cut the cardboard to fit any size or shape you need. Once the cardboard has broken down—usually in 3 months to 6 months, depending on weather conditions— it should be safe enough for you to plant nonaggressive plants in the empty spaces.

Look beyond the plant's original location to be sure you get all of the offending plant.

A cardboard barrier will help prevent a reoccurrence of the problem plant.

BEFORE A rhododendron dominates the bed.

AFTER Cutting the rhododendron back allows the other plants to come into focus.

BEFORE

OVERHAUL AN OVERGROWN TREE OR SHRUB

Sometimes a single plant can begin to dominate a garden bed, and it's hard to decide whether to prune it or remove it. But when a plant starts leaning on its neighbors or growing over a walkway, it's time to take action. If the plant has behaved well in an area for many years and has just grown too big over time, then rejuvenation pruning can get things back under control. If, however, your shrub seems to explode with new growth each year or its natural habit is one that no longer works in the spot, it's best to cut your losses and replace the plant with something more appropriate for the site.

PRUNE

Plants respond differently to pruning, so start by researching whether your plant resprouts easily when cut back or whether it should be pruned a little at a time. Rhododendrons (*Rhododendron* spp. and cvs., USDA Hardiness Zones 3–9), like the one in the bed shown in the photos above and left, respond extraordinarily well to vigorous pruning. Cut the plant back by at least half its overall height so that it no longer dominates the bed.

REMOVE THE PLANT

Some plants, unfortunately, don't like to be pruned. If you have a rock rose (*Cistus* spp. and cvs., Zones 8–11), juniper (*Juniperus* spp. and cvs., Zones 2–9), lavender (*Lavendula* spp. and cvs., Zones 5–9), or rosemary (*Rosmarinus officinalis* and cvs., Zones 8–11) that is overgrowing its space, consider removing it because these plants resent drastic pruning and will never fully recover. While it can be sad to remove a plant, look at it as a great excuse to visit the nursery and research slower-growing alternatives. If you think you'll miss your old plant, you can always take a cutting and put it in another area of the garden. While you wait for the replacement to fill in (or for the severely pruned plant to recover), you can use fast-growing annuals or tropicals to fill the visual hole.

✓ LOW-MAINTENANCE IDEAS
✓ PLANTS FOR SUN
✓ PLANTS FOR SHADE

No garden is complete without low-growing accents like this 'Kim's Knee High' purple coneflower.

✳

PERENNIALS
FOR THE EDGE

Proving that good things do come in small packages, Fine Gardening *contributing editor Stephanie Cohen recommends short and sweet plants for the sunny and shady edges of your beds.*

MANY YEARS AGO, WHEN I FIRST SPOKE AT A WELL-ATTENDED perennial conference, the person introducing me asked if someone had a box because I'm so "vertically challenged." Short people always seem to be the butt of jokes and, in the words of the late comedian Rodney Dangerfield, "get no respect." Not long after that conference, I recognized that short perennials were in the same boat. Large plants seem to get all the accolades. They're often labeled as big, bodacious focal points and are celebrated for their superior architectural effects and textural features. The best that most gardeners have to say about plants for the front of the garden is that they're short; diminutive; small-statured; or, heaven forbid, dwarf—a word that implies misshapen, which most edging perennials are anything but.

No garden is complete without low-growing plants, which beautifully accentuate bed lines, define path and bed boundaries, soften harsh edges, and counter large-scale plants for visual interest. To be worthy of being planted in my garden, perennial edgers have to work hard. They must flower for a long time, have interesting foliage color and texture from spring to fall, and show minimal disease and pest problems.

'Golden Fleece' goldenrod

'Fanfare' blanket flower

'Countess Helen von Stein' lambs' ears

The ideal height of edging plants depends on how close you will be to the beds when viewing them. For beds that are viewed from a distance, 2-foot-tall plants work well. Of course, you can go taller than 2 feet if the plant is see through (or airy enough to permit a view of the plants behind it). For beds that are observed up close, plants that are no more than 18 inches tall fit the bill. No matter where you view them from, the number of good candidates for sun and shade seems almost endless.

PINT-SIZE PLANTS FOR SUN

One of the simplest ways to tie a garden together is to use repetition. This can be done in a number of ways, such as by selecting plants with similar colors and forms. I like to use repetition by echoing traditional perennials with their shorter counterparts.

CONEFLOWERS Classic purple coneflowers (*Echinacea purpurea* and cvs., USDA Hardiness Zones 3–9) typically grow to 3 feet or taller and work well for this approach. While the compact cultivars are not lilliputian, they average 18 inches tall. The smallish 'Kim's Knee High' (see the photo on p. 78) flaunts typical purple-rose blooms, 'Kim's Mop Head' produces white flowers, and 'Little Giant' has larger, purplish blooms with horizontal petals that are supported on 16-inch-tall stems.

All of these cultivars flower in summer and continue until frost with deadheading. They grow in full sun and average soil, and can handle summer heat without looking bedraggled. Their coarse, hairy leaves are rarely bothered by deer, but our four-legged foes often find the flowers palatable. Besides being excellent edgers, short purple coneflowers also attract butterflies and make superb cut flowers.

SHASTA DAISY Another beloved plant with miniaturized sidekicks is the summer-blooming Shasta daisy (*Leucanthemum* × *superbum* cvs., Zones 5–8). My two favorite petite cultivars are 'Snowcap', a Blooms of Bressingham selection, and 'Little Miss Muffet', an older variety. 'Little Miss Muffet' is 12 inches tall, whereas 'Snowcap' reaches 15 inches tall. 'Snowcap' seems to bloom a few weeks longer, especially with deadheading, and is more tolerant of adverse weather conditions. Both of these single white cultivars require full sun and well-drained garden loam. A good use of flower repetition finds the stellar 3-foot-tall 'Becky' Shasta daisy a hop, skip, and a jump from 'Snowcap' or 'Little Miss Muffet'.

SUN LOVERS

PLANT NAME	ZONES	HEIGHT
'ANGELINA' STONECROP (*Sedum rupestre* 'Angelina')	6–9	6 in.
'BLUE ICE' BLUESTAR (*Amsonia* 'Blue Ice')	4–9	14 in.
'BLUE STAR' FALSE ASTER (*Kalimeris incisa* 'Blue Star')	5–9	15 in.
'CARADONNA' SAGE (*Salvia nemorosa* 'Caradonna')	5–9	24 in.
CATMINT (*Nepeta* × *faassenii* cvs.)	4–8	12–24 in.
CLUMP VERBENA (*Verbena* 'Homestead Purple')	6–9	10 in.
DWARF CARDINAL FLOWER (*Lobelia* × *speciosa* 'Grape Knee-High')	5–8	22 in.
DWARF FOUNTAIN GRASS (*Pennisetum alopecuroides* 'Hameln')	6–9	24 in.
DWARF WILLOW-LEAVED SUNFLOWER (*Helianthus salicifolius* 'Low Down')	6–9	12 in.
'FANFARE' BLANKET FLOWER (*Gaillardia* × *grandiflora* 'Fanfare')	3–8	10 in.
'FIRE WITCH' PINK (*Dianthus* 'Fire Witch', syn. *D.* 'Feuerhexe')	3–10	6 in.
'GOLDEN FLEECE' GOLDENROD (*Solidago sphacelata* 'Golden Fleece')	5–9	18 in.
JAPANESE ONION (*Allium thunbergii* 'Ozawa')	4–8	9–12 in.
'KIM'S KNEE HIGH' PURPLE CONEFLOWER (*Echinacea purpurea* 'Kim's Knee High')	3–9	18 in.
LAMBS' EAR (*Stachys byzantina* and cvs.)	4–8	12–18 in.
'LUCERNE' BLUE-EYED GRASS (*Sisyrinchium angustifolium* 'Lucerne')	3–8	12 in.
PLUMBAGO (*Ceratostigma plumbaginoides*)	5–9	18 in.
PRAIRIE POPPY MALLOW (*Callirhoe involucrate*)	4–9	12 in.
'PURPLE DOME' ASTER (*Aster novae-angliae* 'Purple Dome')	4–8	18 in.
'SNOWCAP' SHASTA DAISY (*Leucanthemum* × *superbum* 'Snowcap')	5–8	15 in.
'STEPHANIE RETURNS' DAYLILY (*Hemerocallis* 'Stephanie Returns')	3–8	18 in.
STOKES' ASTER (*Stokesia laevis* and cvs.)	5–9	12–24 in.

BLANKET FLOWERS Blanket flowers (*Gaillardia* × *grandiflora* cvs., Zones 3–8) and I used to mix like oil and water. They always seemed to develop urban sprawl by the time they reached full bloom, creating an ugly mess. Ever since the newer, shorter cultivars came out, however, blanket flowers are again welcome in my garden. Reaching 10 inches tall, the new plants do not flop, and their red-and-yellow blooms produce a riot of color from summer until frost. The selection 'Arizona Sun' has hypnotic flat red flowers edged in yellow. 'Fanfare' has a more unusual look with its fused, trumpetlike red petals with yellow tips (see the center photo on the facing page). Like the rest of

'Ozawa' Japanese onion

'Walker's Low' catmint

'Caradonna' sage

their kin, both plants are drought tolerant and have a long season of bloom, which can increase in abundance with deadheading. For those gardeners looking for something a little more subtle, 'Summer's Kiss' is a dreamy selection that boasts blooms in shades of yellow-apricot.

SAGE *Salvia nemorosa* 'Marcus' and 'Caradonna' are two sages that can easily be the stars of the late-spring border in Zones 5 to 9. 'Marcus' is a compact, 10-inch-tall plant that is covered with violet-blue flower spikes when in bloom. 'Caradonna' has beautiful dark violet spikes, which rise above dramatic deep purple, upright stems that look black when backlit (see the bottom photo on p. 80). Even though 'Caradonna' is about 2 feet tall, its linear, see-through flowers make it a prime contender for the front of the border. Both 'Marcus' and 'Caradonna' require full sun, average garden soil, and good drainage. They're blooming fools well into late summer, especially with deadheading.

For late-season interest, look to *Allium thunbergii* 'Ozawa' (Zones 4–8), which is commonly called the Japanese onion (see the top photo on p. 80). At 9 inches to 12 inches tall, it has strappy, grasslike leaves in summer and bears star-shaped, violet-pink flowers in fall. It grows in almost any garden soil and is not browsed by deer. Because 'Ozawa' flowers late, I place it among plants that bloom earlier in the season to create a succession of color. Of course, there are many spring- and summer-blooming ornamental onions that are suitable for the front of the border. But beware—their foliage does yellow and disappear shortly after flowers fade.

PETITE PERENNIALS FOR SHADE

Sun-loving perennials aren't the only ones with smallish counterparts; shady perennials have their fair share, too.

DWARF WILD COLUMBINE One of the most notable is the dwarf wild columbine 'Little Lanterns', a shorter version of the 3-foot-tall native wild columbine (*Aquilegia canadensis*, Zones 3–8). At 12 inches to 18 inches tall, the midspring to midsummer blooms of 'Little Lanterns' are a more intense red and yellow than the species and sit atop red stems. Its compact habit makes it a good choice for formal shade gardens.

Like its predecessor, 'Little Lanterns' is an important food source for hummingbirds in early spring. It also tends to be deer resistant but not 100 percent deerproof.

'King of Hearts' bleeding heart

It's ideally suited to partial to full shade; however, it can take full sun when sited in moist soil. 'Little Lanterns' can suffer from leaf miner but to a lesser extent than other columbines. I usually just snip off the bad leaves or pretend I didn't see them. If you can't find 'Little Lanterns' and you stumble upon 'Canyon Vista', go for it. The two plants are pretty much identical.

HYBRID BLEEDING HEART Because many spring bloomers fade into nothing after flowering, it's always refreshing to find ones that keep on going. There is a hybrid bleeding heart called 'King of Hearts' (*Dicentra* 'King of Hearts', Zones 5–9; see the top photo at right) that is well deserving of its name. In spring, it lights up the garden with dark rose flowers floating above lacy gray-green leaves. Unlike many other *Dicentra* species and cultivars, 'King of Hearts' is sterile and continues to flower into fall as long as it gets adequate moisture and well-drained garden loam.

In northern climates, site 'King of Hearts' in morning sun and afternoon shade. In southern regions, protect plants from heat and intense sun by placing them in light to medium shade. At 8 inches to 10 inches tall, 'King of Hearts' makes an excellent low-growing specimen at the edge of borders. There is also a white everblooming bleeding heart called *Dicentra* 'Ivory Hearts' (Zones 5–9), which grows to 12 inches tall.

HEUCHERAS Unfortunately, most shade-loving perennials will not give us a lengthy season of bloom like the new bleeding hearts. So to get the most bang for my buck, I choose plants with attractive, long-lasting foliage texture and color. Heucheras (*Heuchera* spp. and cvs., Zones 3–8) are at the top of my list.

Also known as coral bells because of their pinkish white to coral blooms, this clan of perennials has a mounding habit that reaches 12 inches to 18 inches tall. Their most popular feature is their heart-shaped or rounded leaves with ruffled edges that come in a rainbow of colors from purple, green, metallic, and amber—purple being the most prevalent. Newer cultivars offer even more color options. 'Lime Rickey' (Zones 4–9), which sends up pure white flowers in spring, has wonderful chartreuse leaves that fade to lime green by midsummer (see the center photo at right). 'Marmalade' (Zones 4–9), another notable newbie, dazzles the eye with its dramatic umber to sienna leaves with hot pink undersides.

'Lime Rickey' heuchera

Astilbe

TOP LEFT 'Iron Butterfly' foamflower

ABOVE 'Stairway to Heaven' Jacob's ladder

LEFT European wild ginger

Heucheras need moisture-retentive, well-drained soil to thrive. In northern climates, they benefit from morning sun, but in the south, they do better in filtered to medium shade. From a design perspective, they work just about anywhere. They play nicely with other perennials, can hold their own in a massed planting, and are also happy in containers.

BETHLEHEM SAGE Bethlehem sage or lungwort (*Pulmonaria* spp. and cvs., Zones 2–8) is another perennial foliage favorite. Often used as an edger or low-growing focal point, it's valued for its hairy, silver-spotted leaves that shimmer in the shade garden and are not browsed by deer. Lungwort's trumpet-shaped flowers range from blue, white, or pink to deep raspberry and last for a few weeks in spring. Garden-worthy selections include the 12-inch-tall 'Victorian Brooch', which has lovely magenta-coral blooms that grace its long silver leaves for up to two months, and the 8-inch-tall 'Baby Blue', whose flowers start out pink and mature to blue.

Lungworts need moist yet well-drained soil to stand up to the blazing days of summer. They are no stranger to powdery mildew in hot, humid climates, so it's best to choose resistant varieties (like those mentioned here) and give plants some elbow room to promote air circulation. The leaves can be treated with a fungicide or removed once infected; however, because powdery mildew doesn't kill the plants, my strategy is benign neglect. This affliction usually goes unnoticed because it's camouflaged by the lungwort's silvery leaves. This is particularly true of the 12-inch-tall cultivars 'Silver Streamers' and 'Cotton Cool', whose upright leaves are nearly pure silver.

VARIEGATED JACOB'S LADDER The last plant on the hit parade is a new cultivar, which comes to us from the New England Wild Flower Society, called variegated Jacob's ladder (*Polemonium reptans* 'Stairway to Heaven', Zones 3–7). In early spring, the 15-inch-tall plant emerges with green leaves edged in white and tinged pink. Its pale blue flowers appear shortly after and dangle in drooping clusters (see the right photo above). When the flowers begin to fade in early summer, so does the pink hue of the leaves, which makes the white margins seem more pronounced.

Unlike its popular close relative *P. caeruleum*, 'Stairway to Heaven' withstands heat and humidity as well as the

SHADE LOVERS

PLANT NAME	ZONES	HEIGHT
ASTILBES (*Astilbe* spp. and cvs.)	3–8	12–24 in.
AUTUMN FERN (*Dryopteris erythrosora*)	5–9	24 in.
'BABY BLUE' LUNGWORT (*Pulmonaria* 'Baby Blue')	2–8	8 in.
BRUNNERAS (*Brunnera macrophylla* and cvs.)	3–7	15–18 in.
CRANESBILL (*Geranium* spp. and cvs.)	4–8	6–30 in.
DEADNETTLE (*Lamium* spp. and cvs.)	4–8	8–24 in.
DWARF SOLOMON'S SEAL (*Polygonatum humile*)	5–8	8 in.
DWARF WILD COLUMBINE (*Aquilegia canadensis* 'Little Lanterns')	3–8	12–18 in.
EUROPEAN WILD GINGER (*Asarum europaeum*)	4–8	3–6 in.
FOAMFLOWER (*Tiarella* spp. and cvs.)	3–9	4–24 in.
GOATSBEARD (*Aruncus aethusifolius*)	3–9	12 in.
HARDY BEGONIA (*Begonia grandis* ssp. *evansiana*)	6–9	24 in.
HEUCHERELLAS (*Heucherella* cvs.)	5–8	16–24 in.
JAPANESE FOREST GRASS (*Hakonechloa macra* cvs.)	6–9	20 in.
'KING OF HEARTS' BLEEDING HEART (*Dicentra* 'King of Hearts')	5–9	8–10 in.
'LIME RICKEY' HEUCHERA (*Heuchera* 'Lime Rickey')	4–9	12–18 in.
PIGSQUEAK (*Bergenia* spp. and cvs.)	3–9	12–24 in.
SEDGE (*Carex* spp. and cvs.)	3–9	2–30 in.
SNOWDROP ANEMONE (*Anemone sylvestris* and cvs.)	3–9	18 in.
TOAD LILY (*Tricyrtis formosana* and cvs.)	6–9	24 in.
VARIEGATED JACOB'S LADDER (*Polemonium reptans* 'Stairway to Heaven')	3–7	15 in.
WILD STONECROP (*Sedum ternatum*)	4–8	6 in.

cold. It requires moisture-retentive, well-drained soil. It thrives in filtered light or partial shade but will tolerate sunny spots as long as the soil remains moist. 'Stairway to Heaven' works well as a ground cover along walkways and paths. Pair it with other foliage plants that will accent and mirror its early pink tones and white variegation.

While there are many big, whopping perennials that get a lot of the glory, don't forget that the little guys are important, too. No other plants can trim beds and borders or soften hard lines the way these gems can. With plenty to choose from for the sun or shade, vertically challenged perennials always get my respect.

TIPS FOR SHAPING THE LAWN
TO FIT THE GARDEN

Too often, gardeners create planting beds in their yard without paying attention to the lawn shapes that result. Bed and lawn shapes need to be developed in unison so that the two are visually related and in proportion. The lawn, after all, is the setting for our gardens and should not be treated as an afterthought. Fortunately, lawn can be easily removed with a straight-nosed spade, so it's not hard to fix an ill-proportioned lawn and the poorly shaped beds that come of it. Each property is unique, but ensuring that the lawn's shape and size suit the features that surround it invariably creates a pleasing, well-proportioned space.

SET THE SCALE

Though we may not realize it, people instinctively prefer objects that are in proportion to one another over those that are not. So it follows that a lawn area in proportion to the size of existing features, such as planting beds or built structures, is naturally more pleasing to the eye. When assessing your garden space, use the following features to set the scale for your lawn:

- Walls (house, shed, and garage)
- Garden structures (gazebos, arbors, and pergolas)
- Tree trunks or drip lines
- Fences and hedges
- Driveways, paths, and walkways
- Nearby planting beds you don't intend to change

With this information in hand, you can create a well-proportioned lawn and garden space.

PROBLEM
The arbitrary shape of the lawn holds no relationship with the surrounding beds and hardscape.

REWORK A FENCED BACKYARD

In the drawing on the facing page, the size and shape of the lawn, produced by the arbitrary curves of the borders that make them too skinny in some places and too wide in others, fit neither the height nor the shape of the walls. An equally proportioned relationship between the wall, beds, and lawn can be created by measuring out an equal distance—in this case, one-third of the overall width of the garden, or 12 feet—from the stone walls to set new edges for the border. This establishes a pleasing balance between the lawn shape and the existing features.

By measuring out the same distance from the existing tree set within the lawn area, proportional dimensions can be determined even where there is no wall to use as a reference.

If you remove lawn outside the measured edges, then the final result is a well-proportioned ellipse of lawn (see the drawing below). Every element is in proportion and fits together. Complete the design by adding stepping-stones in the border to provide access to this space.

SOLUTION
Establish a balance between the lawn shape and existing features by measuring out an equal distance from existing features.

Add stepping-stones for access.

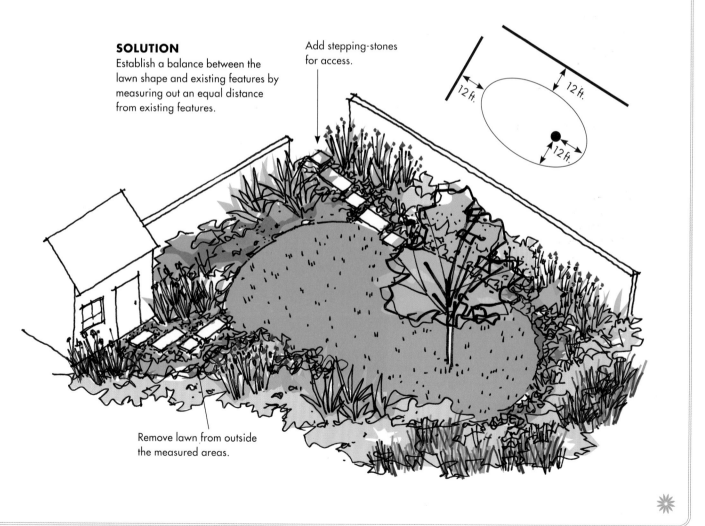

12 ft.

12 ft.

12 ft.

Remove lawn from outside the measured areas.

MIX IT UP
WITH SEE-THROUGH PLANTS

Landscape designer Bobbie Schwartz adds intrigue to staid beds by placing tall, airy perennials up front to give lushness to the garden. She shares how to choose the right plants to create this whimsical effect.

AS A LANDSCAPE DESIGNER, I AM ALWAYS LOOKING FOR unusual ways to combine plants. As part of my design work, I frequently see gardens that feel static because plants are placed in a somewhat rigid manner—that is, short plants in the front, medium plants in the middle, and large or tall plants in the back. One way I break up the monotony of this grammar-school-photo approach to design is to move medium and tall plants to the front or middle of a border. The plants I choose for this placement must, of course, be open in nature so you can see through them. Tall, ornamental grasses and see-through plants help achieve this look. And with so many varieties to choose from, you are sure to find the ideal type for you garden's needs.

Knautia macedonica combined with ornamental grasses at the center of the border forms a translucent scrim that adds mystery to the design.

LACY PLANTS ACT AS LIVING SCRIMS

A see-through plant, by my definition, is one that acts as a scrim, or a translucent curtain, preventing the viewer from clearly seeing everything behind it. A visitor approaching the garden is enticed to move closer or to wander into the garden for a better look at the plants that are slightly obscured. With this approach to border design, I strive for an atmosphere of adventure and mystery, topped off by a touch of romance that I create with soft colors and lacy plants.

Not every plant that allows a view through it is a successful see-through plant. Giant allium (*Allium giganteum*), for example, has 5-inch spherical blossoms atop pencil-thin 3-foot to 4-foot scapes that reveal the neighboring plantings immediately. You can see through them, but they create no sense of mystery.

THE PERFECT PLANT

An ideal see-through plant has delicate foliage and flowers with a loose growth habit and multiple airy stems that don't completely impede the view of the plants behind them. They typically have strong stems that do not flop or need to be staked. The best see-through plants are usually at least 3 feet tall, so most are summer or fall bloomers. In some cases, shorter plants can work well when they are planted on a hill or in a raised bed so that they are situated at eye level. The width of a see-through plant is irrelevant; it merely determines how many plants you will need to create your illusion.

I have not planted the see-through plants in my garden in any particular pattern. Instead, I've used them intermittently to provide a rhythmic visual flow and to invite the viewer to pause at regular intervals. I like "stuffed" gardens, but too many see-through plants can make a bed seem cluttered. I rarely use see-through plants at corners because a plant with a denser habit is needed in these spots to indicate either a beginning or an end. My preference is to place the first see-through plant at least a few feet down from the beginning of the border, ideally along a garden path, to welcome a leisurely stroll.

AN EFFECTIVE SEE-THROUGH PLANTING

To use see-through plants effectively, it is best to plant large, splashy flowers or foliage behind them. Roses (*Rosa* cvs.), clematis vines (*Clematis* cvs.), daylilies (*Hemerocallis* cvs.), garden phloxes (*Phlox paniculata* cvs.), Shasta daisies (*Leucanthemum × superbum* cvs.), and yellow-foliaged hostas (*Hosta* cvs.) all qualify as show-stopper backdrops. Subtle foil plants get lost in the scrim; instead select bold complementary or contrasting colors, depending on your personal preferences. Keep in mind, though, that strongly contrasting plants are the easiest to see. If complementary colors are used, they should be saturated.

One late-blooming perennial, Russian sage (*Perovskia atriplicifolia*), with its narrow gray-green foliage and spikes of pale lavender, is an asset to any garden, especially when enhanced by a boldly colored plant in the background. Some choices are sneezeweed (*Helenium autumnale*), false sunflowers (*Heliopsis helianthoides* and cvs.), Japanese anemones (*Anemone × hybrida* cvs.), and the annual *Cosmos bipinnatus* 'Sonata Carmine'.

SOME PLEASING PLANT COMBINATIONS

A sun-loving see-through favorite of mine is the 6-foot giant kale (*Crambe cordifolia*). Its airiness keeps it from being overwhelming, even when planted at the front of a border or, in my case, in the middle of a border. While it is blooming, in late spring to early summer, I can easily see a climbing 'William Baffin' rose from one angle and catch a peek of peonies (*Paeonia* spp. and cvs.) and a fellow see-through plant, knautia (*Knautia macedonica*), from another angle.

Chinese and Japanese anemones also act as see-through plants in my garden. These gems, which bloom in late summer to early fall, provide a 3-foot floral scrim. The casual passerby can catch a glimpse of the lavender-pink blooms of my 'Shortwood' garden phlox (*Phlox paniculata* 'Shortwood') behind a loose veil of 'September Charm' and 'Honorine Jobert' anemones (*Anemone hupehensis* 'September Charm' and *A. × hybrida* 'Honorine Jobert').

SHADY AREA PLANTS

In a shaded, narrow bed on the east side of my property, I use bugbane (*Actaea racemosa*), one of my favorite shade perennials. Viewed from the front, its beautiful white spires of delicate blossoms supply a thin veil behind which

TOP Rising above the hedge, the red crocosmia (left) and light purple whisps of Russian sage (right) entice visitors into the garden by offering a glimpse of the plants beyond.

ABOVE The white frill of Japanese anemones draws the eye through to the distant plantings, giving this garden visual depth.

can be seen the blossoms or fluffy seed heads of 'General Sikorski' clematis and a small stand of 'Morden Pink' purple loosestrife (*Lythrum virgatum* 'Morden Pink'), which has not increased in size or seeded in 17 years. Viewed from the side, the billowy white flowers of *Hydrangea arborescens* 'Annabelle' are revealed in all their bounteous glory. This ease of viewing is generally true with spiky perennials like foxgloves (*Digitalis purpurea* and cvs.) and red hot pokers (*Kniphofia uvaria* and cvs.), which allow us to see above the basal foliage and past the thin flower stems and spikes to the plants behind them.

ORNAMENTAL GRASSES

Ornamental grasses are the quintessential see-through plants, and they add two elements to a garden that most other perennials do not. Their upright foliage contributes vertical linearity, and their ability to sway in the wind creates an ever-changing picture.

Of the many grasses I use, my favorite is moor grass (*Molinia caerulea* and cvs.). This grass has foliage that usually grows to 2 feet tall, while the wispy inflorescences can be 7 feet to 8 feet high. This is especially true of the cultivars *M. caerulea* ssp. *arundinacea* 'Windspiel' and *M. caerulea* ssp. *arundinacea* 'Skyracer'. In a bed located just outside my living room window, I planted 'Skyracer', which provides a scrim for my hollyhocks (*Alcea rosea* cvs.), cosmos, and flowering tobaccos (*Nicotiana* spp. and cvs.) from inside as well as from the street.

Although it is not a grass, I would mention fennel (*Foeniculum vulgare* and cvs.) here. Both the species and the cultivar 'Purpureum' make excellent see-through plants. With its feathery foliage and delicate yellow umbels it lends presence to the garden when intermingled with bright orange California and Oriental poppies (*Eschscholzia californica* and *Papaver orientale* cvs.).

I am sure you can compile your own list of see-through plants as you look around your gardens. In doing so, keep in mind that some woodies also make good candidates.

Bugbane (*Actaea racemosa*), with its long-stemmed spiky flowers, permits a view of the plants beyond.

Moor grass caught in the wind provides a delicate curtain of motion against the static lawn.

FAVORITE SEE-THROUGH PLANTS

PLANT NAME	ZONES	FLOWER COLOR	BLOOM TIME
UP TO 4 FEET TALL			
BLACK-LEAVED COW PARSLEY (*Anthriscus sylvestris* 'Ravenswing')	7–10	White	Late spring
SWEET ROCKETS (*Hesperis matronalis* and cvs.)	4–9	White, lilac	Early summer
ORIENTAL FOUNTAIN GRASS (*Pennisetum orientale*)	6–10	Silvery pink	Midsummer
CROCOSMIAS (*Crocosmia* spp. and cvs.)	6–9	Yellow, red, orange	Summer
'KARL FOERSTER' REED GRASS (*Calamagrostis* × *acutiflora* 'Karl Foerster')	5–9	Pale bronzy gold	Summer
CHINESE ANEMONE (*Anemone hupehensis* 'September Charm')	5–7	Pale pink	Summer–fall
KNAUTIA (*Knautia macedonica*)	5–9	Maroon	Summer–frost
HUMMINGBIRD MINT (*Agastache cana*)	6–11	Rose pink	Summer–frost
GAURA (*Gaura lindheimeri* and cvs.)	6–9	White, pink	Summer–fall
PURPLE TOADFLAXES (*Linaria purpurea* and cvs.)	5–8	Lilac, pink	Summer–fall
4 FEET TO 6 FEET TALL			
COMMON FOXGLOVES (*Digitalis purpurea* and cvs.)	4–8	Pink, white	Summer
FENNEL (*Foeniculum vulgare* and cvs.)	4–9	Yellow	Summer
MEADOW RUES (*Thalictrum* spp. and cvs.)	5–9	White, purple, yellow	Summer
MULLEINS (*Verbascum* spp. and cvs.)	3–9	White, yellow	Summer
GAYFEATHERS (*Liatris* spp. and cvs.)	3–9	Purple	Late summer
MOOR GRASSES (*Molinia caerulea* and cvs.)	5–9	Purple	Late summer
RED HOT POKERS (*Kniphofia uvaria* and cvs.)	5–9	Yellow, orange	Late summer
JAPANESE ANEMONE (*Anemone* × *hybrida* 'Honorine Jobert')	4–8	White	Summer–fall
RUSSIAN SAGE (*Perovskia atriplicifolia*)	6–9	Violet-purple	Summer–frost
BLUE BUTTONS (*Knautia arvensis*)	5–9	Bluish purple	Summer–frost
FOUNTAIN GRASSES (*Pennisetum alopecuroides* and cvs.)	6–9	Bronze	Summer–frost
SWITCH GRASSES (*Panicum virgatum* and cvs.)	5–9	Purple, green	Early fall
6 FEET TO 8 FEET TALL			
TALL VERBENA (*Verbena bonariensis*)	7–11	Violet	Summer–frost
GIANT KALE (*Crambe cordifolia*)	6–9	White	Early summer
BUGBANE/BLACK COHOSH (*Actaea racemosa*)	3–8	White	Mid-summer
GIANT FEATHER GRASS (*Stipa gigantea*)	8–11	Gold when ripe	Summer

Ample hardscape and bold plantings create a balance between private and public space, transforming an unremarkable lot into the highlight of the neighborhood.

CREATE A GREAT
FIRST IMPRESSION

New homes often have underdeveloped front yards with little or no personality. Such was the case with homeowner Joy Gregory's new property, so she enlisted designer Rebecca Sams to transform it into a welcoming, attractive landscape.

WHEN JOY GREGORY FOUND HER NEW HOME ON THE OUTSKIRTS of Eugene, Oregon, almost everything fell into place. The quiet, newly constructed development was filled with young families like Joy's. She liked the house, the neighborhood, and the community, but she couldn't say the same about her front yard.

The only way to enter the property was from the driveway, and there was no aesthetic appeal to the scrappy lawn and sparse foundation plantings. The scale of the house and driveway made the 900-square-foot area seem even smaller, and what little privacy the wide driveway and proximity of the street might have allowed was lost with the next-door neighbor's front porch just a few feet from Joy's property line.

Well aware of the shortcomings of the property, we set out to create an inviting front-yard garden composed of low-maintenance plantings and a bit of private space Joy and her son could enjoy. Using the disadvantages as guidelines for a design, we set out to improve access to the property, make the scale of the garden fit the house, and increase the purpose and privacy within the space to turn this unsightly afterthought into a beautiful front yard.

Foliage means less fuss than flowers, as the burgundy, bronze, silver, and cream variegation echo the hardscape palette of this sandstone path.

IMPROVING ACCESS IS THE FIRST STEP

The challenge of this project was to turn a front yard with no strong boundaries or organization into a welcoming, distinct, and useful garden. By using ample pathways, distinct materials, and a striking focal feature, we enlivened the space, giving the garden purpose and interest.

Improving access was our first priority. Broad pathways attract the eye and invite guests to explore, and a new 6-foot-wide sandstone path that delivers visitors directly from the sidewalk to the front door does just that. Three broad steps emphasize a small grade change, defining the garden as a space distinct from the street.

The family still needed a convenient driveway entrance, but we made a few improvements. We replaced the narrow concrete path that skirted the garage wall from the driveway with a sandstone path. The change in material emphasizes the distinct quality of this transitional area, and the short, utilitarian path engages the eye as bold plantings around it frame the view of a large Vietnamese urn and adjacent seating area.

Both access paths, from the sidewalk and the driveway, are centered on the Vietnamese urn, planted to the brim with flowers and foliage. This important focal feature captures attention from every angle, anchoring the hardscape to the garden, while its elegant form and color add interest and energy to the scene.

MAKE A SMALL SPACE FEEL BIG

As in similar housing developments, the original foundation plantings did not match the size of the house's two-story facade, and the driveway was almost as large as the front yard. The small amount of space available for a garden was overwhelmed by the surrounding architectural elements. This disadvantage, however, became a great opportunity. Rather than match the design to the scale of the diminutive front yard, the bold hardscape, features, and plantings were selected to fit the size of the house and driveway.

The path and stairs from the street are broad enough to command notice but narrow enough to maintain focus on the Vietnamese urn inside the garden. Visitors are drawn into, rather than around, the garden by the engaging combination of the urn and hardscape set to a large scale.

The wide, open areas near the entrance to the house, around the urn, and at the seating area make the garden comfortable, inviting, and functional. Guests linger on the central terrace, and Joy loves to relax on the stone bench while her son plays in the garden.

There is a temptation to use small plants in a small space because they take up less room. Instead of being limited by a lack of square footage on the ground, however, we laid claim to the abundant cubic footage above the ground. A large specimen 'Saratoga' ginkgo (*Ginkgo biloba* 'Saratoga', USDA Hardiness Zones 5–9) and weeping giant redwoods (*Sequoiadendron giganteum* 'Pendulum', Zones 6–9) soften the facade of the house by rising up to match its size while taking up little ground space.

PLANT IN MASSES

Enjoy lush plantings without the hassle of constant upkeep.

- Large groups add impact yet reduce the amount of work per square foot.
- Plants with different flowering periods used en masse divide the task of deadheading into a few periods of focused work.
- Large swaths of ornamental grasses provide a long-term foil for surrounding plants yet need to be cut back only once a year.

Wide paths balance the scale of the hardscape and the planting beds. Richly colored materials that match the plant palette make this design look and feel right.

The more-up-than-out philosophy is useful in small gardens and does not stop with the specimen trees. New Zealand flax (*Phormium* spp. and cvs., Zones 8–11) and ornamental grasses, such as 'Karl Foerster' feather reed grass (*Calamagrostis* × *acutiflora* 'Karl Foerster', Zones 5–9) are a step shorter than trees but still provide good screening when massed. These tall plants, combined with colorful ground covers, give texture, depth, and privacy to the garden.

BALANCING PURPOSE AND PRIVACY

Balancing privacy with the desire for a welcoming feeling adds another layer of complexity to any front-yard design, and finding a comfortable location for a seating area in this tiny plot wasn't easy. Limitations, however, can guide you to unique and beautiful solutions.

We searched for a space that would be surrounded by the garden yet removed from the main pathways, and discovered that the best spot for a bench was a nook near the property line, just feet from the neighbors' front porch. Obviously, screening was a priority, and we

LEFT Strong colors engage the eye. Bold plants, like the cream-colored euphorbia (*Euphorbia characias* 'Tasmanian Tiger', Zones 7–10), draw visitors up the path.

BELOW A bench makes the space useful. Only inches from the property line, this nook ensures that the front garden isn't just a space to walk through.

scratched our heads over how to create a private space that would retain the breezy, playful atmosphere of the rest of the garden without walling off more space than was necessary with a fence or hedge. Our solution was a 6-foot-high by 9-foot-wide rusting metal screen set along the property line, perpendicular to the street. A strong visual barrier, it adds privacy and rich color to the seating area but extends only inches beyond the edges of the stone terrace. The garden between the seating area and the street is filled with plants of varying heights, textures, and forms, creating a soft border in the playful style of the garden.

Selecting the right materials, scale, and forms for this design created a visual harmony that resonates beyond this small space. Friends now linger in the front yard, and neighborhood kids play on the garden steps. Every element engages the family and its visitors in a space that would normally be overlooked. This family's front garden is now accessible, functional, beautiful, and, most important, part of the home.

It's different, but it still fits in. When driving by this front yard in Knoxville, Tennessee, it's obvious that a gardener lives inside. But when creating the space, the owner took deliberate steps to maintain continuity with the rest of the less colorful neighborhood.

✓ ADD COLOR
✓ DESIGN IDEAS
✓ ECO-FRIENDLY OPTION
✓ PLANT SUGGESTIONS

STAND OUT
WITHOUT STICKING OUT

Tired of caring for a high-maintenance lawn, homeowner Faye Beck remade her front yard into a gardener's dream while keeping it connected with its surroundings. Professors of horticulture Sue Hamilton and Andy Pulte tell you how she did it.

DRIVE DOWN ANY SUBURBAN STREET ACROSS THE COUNTRY, AND you're likely to see the same old thing: lawn, lawn, lawn, spruce tree, lawn. This would be a dream come true for early landscape architects, like Frederick Law Olmsted, who saw a nonstop sea of grass as a way to bind houses together in a parklike setting. Since those early days, the lawn has been seen as a way of establishing an instant relationship with the neighbors—a relationship built on our mingling turfs. A nice lawn can be a beautiful thing, but if you are a gardener, this monotony is not a dream but a nightmare.

Most gardeners want an exuberant front yard that is overflowing with plants. This, unfortunately, would surely make their landscape stick out like a sore thumb from their neighbors'. So how can gardeners set their residence apart without making it look like a rowdy front-yard circus with no connection to its surroundings? Faye Beck's 5,000-square-foot garden is the perfect example of a successful design that embraces the middle ground. By using three specific strategies, Faye formed a unique front-yard landscape that manages to say, "Yes, a gardener does live here—but I still fit in."

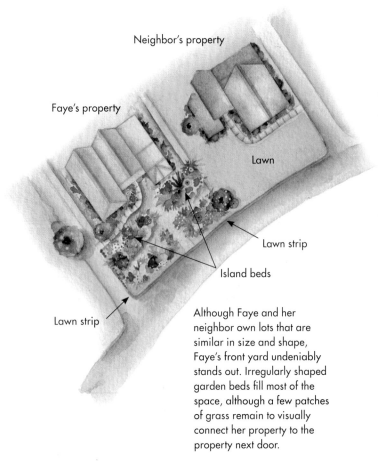

Neighbor's property

Faye's property

Lawn

Lawn strip

Island beds

Lawn strip

Although Faye and her neighbor own lots that are similar in size and shape, Faye's front yard undeniably stands out. Irregularly shaped garden beds fill most of the space, although a few patches of grass remain to visually connect her property to the property next door.

KEEP JUST ENOUGH GRASS FOR EFFECT

Tired of looking at and caring for her high-maintenance front lawn, Faye decided to install several garden beds. During their installation, she wanted to get rid of the lawn completely. But ripping out all of the turf was too drastic and would have put her front landscape at odds with the rest of the neighborhood. Faye, instead, left a few areas of grass along her front curb and along the property lines she shares with neighbors. These grassy spots help maintain a connection to the surrounding homes and are easily mowed with a string trimmer.

The best part is that the lawn sections are visible only from the street. Faye doesn't have to look at them from her front door, but passersby on the street think that there are more areas of turf beyond the eye's reach. This makes Faye's yard seem less out of place in her turf-heavy neighborhood. As a bonus, Faye no longer needs to worry about fighting lawn weeds or diseases. She even plans to replace the remaining patches of turf with dwarf mondo grass (*Ophiopogon japonicus* 'Nana', USDA Hardiness Zones 7–10), which will look like lawn but will not have to be mowed, fertilized, or treated with herbicides.

Turf plays a small but important role. Because most of the neighborhood has a traditional front lawn, keeping a little grass along the edge of the garden beds was crucial so that this property didn't seem foreign in its surroundings.

LEFT Forget about straight lines. When designing a small space, curved beds make a garden seem large and, in turn, full. This planting, which stretches between the front walkway and the house foundation, doesn't appear to end, although when it is actually only 25 feet long.

BELOW Color helps move the eye. Plants with similar hues, like this black-eyed Susan (*Rudbeckia* cv., Zones 3–11), coleus (*Solenostemon scutellarioides* cv., Zone 11), and 'Fireworks' fountain grass (*Pennisetum* 'Fireworks', Zones 9–10), give a design fluidity.

GIVE THE ILLUSION OF MORE SPACE

Lawns generally feel and look spacious, so Faye needed to avoid creating a garden that looked and felt claustrophobic. She initially built long, traditional borders in her front yard but then decided to slowly expand them into irregularly shaped, slightly bermed islands. Expanding the beds not only provided room for more plants but also gave the front yard a greater sense of space. Straight lines tell the eye to stop, whereas curved lines trick the eye into thinking that the expanse goes on indefinitely. To give the beds distinct edges, which can sometimes be a challenge with curved beds, Faye used fieldstone and river rock.

Although Faye's front garden is only 5,000 square feet, visitors are always amazed by the variety of views they experience while traveling the paths between her beds. Everywhere you look, you try to anticipate what Faye has hidden around the deliberate curves. The nonlinear shapes of the beds also lend a sense of informality to the garden, allowing Faye an almost limitless plant palette. Placing large plants in the middle of the beds—instead of off to one side—allows visitors to enjoy them from every angle because they must walk around the perimeter to take it all in.

CONNECT THE COLORS

With thousands of plants to choose from, how do you select the ones for your beds? Faye's process involved, first, picking a focal plant, then creating waves of color echoes based on that plant. Here's how the process works:

1 'Australia' canna (*Canna* 'Australia', Zones 8–11)
This canna is the starter plant—a towering clump that is the main focal point of the bed.

2 'Religious Radish' coleus (*Solenostemon scutellarioides* 'Religious Radish', Zone 11)
The bright red tip of the coleus leaves perfectly matches the flowers of the nearby canna.

3 'Tomato Soup' coneflower (*Echinacea* 'Tomato Soup', Zones 4–9)
The center cones of these blossoms echo the deep burgundy of the canna leaves.

4 Margaritaville™ yucca (*Yucca recurvifolia* 'Hinvargas', Zones 7–11)
Drawing inspiration from the vibrant green foliage of the cuphea, Faye planted a variegated yucca next to it because of its distinctive green leaf margin.

5 'Flamenco Samba' cuphea (*Cuphea llavea* 'Flamenco Samba', Zones 8–10)
This cuphea is a self-sower that surrounds the cone-flower, and its blossom color is just a shade lighter than that of 'Tomato Soup'.

6 'Dwarf Bright Gold' Japanese yew (*Taxus cuspidata* 'Dwarf Bright Gold', Zones 5–7)
The golden needles of this conifer complement the subtle yellow tones of the yucca blades.

7 Leatherleaf sedge (*Carex buchananii*, Zones 6–9)
The brown leatherleaf sedge picks up the smoky bronze tones of the sword-shaped crocosmia leaves.

8 'Solfatare' crocosmia (*Crocosmia* 'Solfatare', Zones 6–9)
When in bloom, the honey-colored flowers of this perennial are even more eye-catching with the golden-leaved yew as a backdrop.

PLANT IN BLOCKS OF COLOR

Being a savvy gardener, Faye created a mixed garden
by filling in her beds with a little of everything: dwarf
conifers, trees, shrubs, ornamental grasses, perennials,
tropicals, bulbs, and annuals. But her approach to
blending different plant materials together was guided
by color. As she slowly extended the footprint of her
beds, she selected companions that would allow her to
create drifts of color. If, for instance, a canna (*Canna*
spp. and cvs., Zones 8–11) were firmly established in a
bed, she selected a companion that possessed one of the
canna-leaf hues (see "Connect the Colors" on the facing
page). Then she isolated a different color aspect of the
companion plant to find a buddy for it, planting the
buddy to one side.

   This method of combining plants created waves of
colors in Faye's garden that help move the eye from one
area to the next and give the front garden a sense of

Make the space exciting but not peculiar. The goal of
creating a distinctive front garden is for it to look like
the colorful cousin of the neighborhood. The garden
should relate to the community as a whole without
abandoning any of the garden's flair.

continuity. Every part of a plant is fair game for color
matching: leaves, seed heads, flowers, and even emerging
growth or fading blossoms. Faye points out, however, that
you can't just combine plants that look great together;
they have to share the same cultural requirements.

   As visitors pass by Faye's front yard, they know
instantly that a gardener lives on the property.
And although it is not the typical landscape in her
neighborhood, it still belongs, which makes Faye—and
her neighbors—happy.

Elise Warnstaff's streetside garden in Portland, Oregon, provides multiseason interest with evergreen shrubs and long-blooming perennials.

STREETWISE PLANTINGS

That strip of grass between the road and the sidewalk may seem like wasted space, but by using tough, colorful plants garden writer C. Colston Burrell shows how to transform it into a garden that will add to your home's curb appeal.

FRONT YARDS ARE WHERE FIRST AND LASTING IMPRESSIONS ARE made. Like it or not, when your garden borders the street, your plantings are in the public eye. And you may be bucking some longstanding conventions. Emerald turf, clipped hedges, and controlled foundation plantings have been de rigueur since they adorned Colonial Williamsburg.

Urban and suburban landscapes of North America still reflect this design tradition, which was cemented in the postwar era. Beginning in the mid-1940s, rampant development led to cookie-cutter subdivisions. The velvet greensward we call lawn still has a stranglehold on the American imagination—but not for long. Gardeners are breaking from tradition and taking back the front yard as a canvas for personal expression. Perhaps the most visible examples of this trend are plantings that go right up to the street.

As early as the 1970s, inspired by the environmental movement, a few innovators traded in their front turf for more colorful and interesting plantings. This trend began in the Midwest and on the West Coast, and has spread throughout North America.

ABOVE Front-yard gardens extend gardening space on small city lots. The author planted prairie plants in his former boulevard garden in Minneapolis.

RIGHT Even seating can be part of a streetside planting. Lucy and Fred Hardiman of Portland, Oregon, created this nook in their front yard to invite passersby to linger.

Today's streetside gardens take many forms, from the ornamental to the utilitarian. Lawns are being redefined or removed to allow for walkways, seating areas, and art objects, as well as plants. Plantings may include shrubs, trees, perennials, herbs, vegetables, bulbs, and ground covers. These new streetwise gardens are welcoming havens.

CONSIDER THE CHALLENGES OF A STREETSIDE SITE

Although gardening along a street or roadway can be rewarding, it has its potential frustrations. Before you take your garden to the street, evaluate the site and any special challenges your plantings might face. How might vehicular and pedestrian traffic affect your plantings? What about snow plows and their attendant salt spray? Are there trees casting shade, or with root systems to accommodate? Must you consider access for public utilities?

The strip between the sidewalk and the street, often called a boulevard or parking strip, can be a great place to make a colorful garden. However, even in urban neighborhoods, where individuality is often celebrated, a streetside planting may raise some eyebrows, or worse, ire. Because such gardens are so public, they are subject to close scrutiny by neighbors, which can generate complaints as well as compliments.

Many cities and subdivisions have weed or nuisance ordinances that prohibit vegetation over a certain arbitrary height, usually 10 inches to 12 inches. Some places even have laws prohibiting boulevard plantings. By virtue of these laws, a governing body can require you to cut down your garden, or at least they can try. You may be able to appeal such rulings, but it's best to know local guidelines and to try to work within them. Though citations are rare when a garden is colorful and well groomed, gardens with native plants, such as prairie plantings, are particularly vulnerable because they may look weedy to uninitiated eyes. One year, my boulevard garden in Minneapolis received a ticket from the weed police just days after I had received a city beautification award. I faxed my award to the office that handles ordinances, and I was able to leave the garden intact.

STREETWORTHY PLANTS

The following are just a few of the resilient, lower-growing plants that work well in streetside plantings.
S = sun, PS = part shade, SH = full shade

NAME	ZONES	HEIGHT & WIDTH	LIGHT
COLUMBINE (*Aquilegia* spp. and cvs.)	3–9	1–3 ft. × 1–2 ft.	S/SH
ARTEMISIA (*Artemisia* spp. and cvs.)	3–9	1–4 ft. × 1–4 ft.	S
BUTTERFLY WEED (*Asclepias tuberosa*)	4–9	1–2 ft. × 1 ft.	S/PS
UPLAND WHITE ASTER (*Aster ptarmicoides*)	3–8	8–10 in. × 12 in.	S/PS
BRONZE SEDGE (*Carex comans* 'Bronze')	7–9	1 ft. × 1–2 ft.	S/PS
WOOD SPURGE (*Euphorbia amygdaloides*)	6–9	12–18 in. × 12–18 in.	PS/SH
MEDITERRANEAN SPURGE (*Euphorbia characias*)	7–10	3–5 ft. × 3 ft.	S/PS
DAYLILY (*Hemerocallis* cvs.)	3–10	1–3 ft. × 1–3 ft.	S/PS
BEARDED IRIS (*Iris* cvs.)	3–9	1–3 ft. × 1–2 ft.	S/PS
LAVENDER (*Lavandula* spp. and cvs.)	5–10	1–2.5 ft. × 1–2.5 ft.	S
BLAZING STAR (*Liatris* spp.)	4–9	2–4 ft. × 1 ft.	S
PURPLE MOOR GRASS (*Molinia caerulea*)	5–9	2–3 ft. × 2–3 ft.	S/PS
DAFFODIL (*Narcissus* cvs.)	3–9	1–2 ft. × 1–2 ft.	S/SH
CATMINT (*Nepeta* spp.)	3–9	1–3 ft. × 1–3 ft.	S
EVENING PRIMROSE (*Oenothera* spp.)	3–9	1–2 ft. × 1–2 ft.	S/PS
RUSSIAN SAGE (*Perovskia atriplicifolia*)	6–9	3–5 ft. × 3–5 ft.	S
STICKY JERUSALEM SAGE (*Phlomis russeliana*)	4–9	2–3 ft. × 3 ft.	S
JERUSALEM SAGE (*Phlomis tuberosa*)	4–8	2–4 ft. × 1–2 ft.	S
MOSS PHLOX (*Phlox subulata*)	3–8	2–6 in. × 20 in.	S/PS
BLACK–EYED SUSAN (*Rudbeckia fulgida*)	3–9	1–2 ft. × 1–2 ft.	S/PS
BLACK–EYED SUSAN (*Rudbeckia hirta*)	3–7	1–2 ft. × 1–2 ft.	S/PS
SAGE (*Salvia* spp. and cvs.)	3–10	1–3 ft. × 1–3 ft.	S
LITTLE BLUESTEM (*Schizachyrium scoparium*)	5–9	2–3 ft. × 1–2 ft.	S
STONECROP AND SEDUM (*Sedum* spp. and cvs.)	3–10	1–3 ft. × 1–3 ft.	S/PS
HENS AND CHICKS (*Sempervivum* spp.)	4–10	2–4 in. × 2–10 in.	S/PS
GRAY GOLDENROD (*Solidago nemoralis*)	3–9	1–2 ft. × 1–2 ft.	S
GOLDENROD (*Solidago sphacelata* 'Golden Fleece')	4–9	1–2 ft. × 1–2 ft.	S
THYME (*Thymus* spp. and cvs.)	4–10	2–6 in. × 1 ft.	S
YUCCA (*Yucca* spp.)	4–10	1–3 ft. × 1–3 ft.	S

STRIVE FOR A COLORFUL AND PRACTICAL PLANTING SCHEME

Because so-called weed ordinances are usually enforced in response to complaints, you're less likely to be cited if your planting looks like a garden. A well-designed streetside planting should show intent and careful tending. People recognize that flowers must be cared for, so a colorful garden with something in bloom from spring through frost will look intentional (see the photo on p. 106).

Though looks are important, consider practical issues as well. For visibility and safety, the mature height of all but an occasional accent plant should be no more than 3 feet. If you garden on a corner lot, taper the plantings down toward the corner so cars can see around the turn, and pedestrians, especially children, are clearly visible. Consider creating borders along edges of a boulevard planting or a cut-through pathway. Make sure you're not restricting access to a fire hydrant or public utility.

There are other things to keep in mind as you design a streetside garden. Fine-textured plants, especially ornamental grasses, may appear weedy to nongardeners. Combine grasses with bulbs, perennials, and shrubs, or try planting them in bold patterns. Plants that hang over the sidewalk will be a nuisance, especially if people must brush against the foliage to pass by.

CHOOSE TOUGH PLANTS

A successful streetside planting must include tough, drought- and salt-tolerant plants that will stand up to the indignation and uninvited intrusions of public life. Plants with bulbs, rhizomes, taproots, and other water-storing structures are excellent choices (see "Streetworthy Plants" on p. 109). Many will go dormant after they flower, so they can tolerate extended dry periods. One approach is to choose drought- and heat-adapted native meadow or prairie plants to reduce maintenance (see the photo below). Ornamental grasses with deep, fibrous roots also thrive despite adversity.

Mediterranean plants are also good choices. Plants with reflective silver and gray foliage, such as *Artemisia* species, lavenders (*Lavandulas* pp.), Jerusalem sages (*Phlomis*

Plants must be tough to live on the street. Lauren Springer used drought-tolerant plants in her boulevard garden near Denver.

Curbside plantings can extend a cottage garden. Bordering a quiet, old street in Atlanta, David Ellis's front garden conveys a sense of informal charm.

russeliana and *P. fruticosa*), and catmints (*Nepeta* spp.) often beat the heat. Succulents and other plants adapted to arid climates, like *Sedum*, *Yucca*, and *Aloe* species and hens and chicks (*Sempervivum* spp.), are good choices where they are hardy. Avoid spiny or thorny plants, which may injure people.

PREPARE THE BED CAREFULLY

Because streetside planting areas are usually far from a spigot, watering may not be easy. Boulevard strips are usually too narrow for conventional sprinklers, and neighbors seldom relish a shower while walking down the street. So proper soil preparation and plant choice are paramount.

CLEAR THE AREA The first step is to kill or remove turfgrass. You can cut away sod with a kick-style sod stripper, dig it by hand with a spading fork, spray it with a glyphosate herbicide like Roundup®, or smother it by covering it with black plastic. If you use an herbicide,

pick a still, warm day when the grass is actively growing. Follow label directions and spray lightly but evenly over the chosen area. The grass will yellow in about 7 days and will be dead in 10 days to 14 days. Glyphosate binds to the soil and quickly breaks down. Killing sod with plastic takes 1 month to 3 months.

You will need to assess the soil, light, and potential moisture conditions of the site to decide which plants will thrive. Generally, streetside soil is poor. It's often compacted and filled with gravel, construction rubble, and tree roots. Remove the upper layer and set it aside in a wheelbarrow or on a tarp. Discard the impoverished subsoil, removing any debris. Watch for broken glass and other sharp edges. Protect your hands with gloves. If you're working around street trees, remember that the roots are a tree's lifeline and are essential to its health.

PLANTING A STREETSIDE GARDEN

Carefully prepare a bed for a streetside planting. After getting rid of the turf in her boulevard strip, Bonnie Blodgett of St. Paul, Minnesota, amended the poor soil with compost and peat (see the top photo at right). Landscape timbers were placed along the street edge to counteract the sloping grade. The fire hydrant was set off with Belgian block and gravel to ensure easy access.

Prairie, Mediterranean, and other tough plants thrive in streetside plantings. To get a bed off to a good start, plant it all at once and add a thick layer of mulch to hold in water and suppress weeds (see the center photo at right). Water new plantings only until they become established. Ideally, streetside gardens should not require supplemental water.

Small starter plants usually grow quickly. After a few months, herbs, grasses, and tough perennials begin to fill in.

TOP When you remove the old turf you also remove salt and other chemicals that have built up in the sod.

MIDDLE Prepare the beds well with mulch now so that they will be easy to care for and look neat later.

BOTTOM If you choose your plants correctly, you should have to water regularly only to establish new plants. After that the goal is a low-maintenance watering plan.

Do your best to work around larger roots, removing what soil you can.

PREP FOR PLANTING Return the topsoil to the planting area, along with amendments, such as manure or compost, to enrich the soil. If the soil is extremely heavy, add a generous amount of sand or tiny gravel as well. If you strip the sod, you may take away your best layer of soil. However, by stripping sod in areas with high snowfall, you will likely remove sand and gravel that has accumulated over years of treating the streets. If you plant native grasses and meadow or prairie plants, you needn't amend the soil for these tough plants unless it's truly inhospitable.

Plan for the finished elevation to remain 3 inches to 4 inches below the curb and sidewalk. This drop allows rainwater to run off the sidewalk and into the planting bed, where it can soak into the ground rather than running down the storm sewer. In areas with high snowfall, it allows space for the sand and other debris to accumulate. If a plow or snow blower should accidentally roll over the area, the crowns of plants will be below grade, thus escaping harm.

PLANT Set plants as you would any containerized nursery stock. Be sure to thoroughly break up the roots before you plant. Due to the rigors of the streetside environment, plugs and small plants may fare better than large, landscape-size stock. Their vigorous new growth will help them adapt more quickly than a full-grown plant with an extensive root system that must readjust to a new situation.

KEEP STREETSIDE PLANTS TIDY

Proper maintenance is critical to the success of streetside plantings. A public streetscape is no place for bedraggled plants or beds cluttered with weeds.

Plants suited to your streetside site should need watering only the first season, while they get established. In subsequent years, they should need little or no supplemental watering, except during extended drought. If you choose a planting scheme that requires regular supplemental water, consider a soaker hose. Because lengths of hose lying on a city sidewalk pose a safety hazard, be vigilant about monitoring the hose.

As for annual maintenance, when I lived in Minneapolis, I left my streetside plantings standing over the winter. They added textural interest and provided wildlife habitat. In spring, I cut down all plants and tidied up. In regions where snow is not persistent, cut back plants when they begin to look disheveled or when a heavy snow flattens them.

When you tidy up, cut all herbaceous plants and grasses to the ground. Round out the crowns of the grass clumps to form a neat cushion 2 inches to 3 inches tall. Prune shrubs to remove dead or damaged growth. Discard fallen leaves or shred them and return them to the beds as mulch. In climates with heavy snowfall, you may find a layer of sand and gravel piled on the beds in spring. Carefully scoop out this debris with a trowel so the crowns of the plants are not buried. When your streetside plantings reappear, you and your neighbors will have another season of front-yard beauty to savor.

MAILBOX GARDEN DESIGN TIPS

A s an American landscape icon, the roadside mailbox is second only to the white picket fence. Your mailbox is probably the first thing passersby and visitors encounter as they approach your home, so a clever design for the garden that surrounds it goes a long way toward setting the tone for the look and feel of your property. For that reason, knowing what it takes to design a good mailbox garden is useful information for nearly every homeowner. Many mailbox gardens, however, are afterthoughts, and they look shabby because people fail to put the same amount of effort into designing them as they do the rest of the garden. You can turn your mailbox into an attractive focal point if you keep in mind a few specific design considerations.

DEEMPHASIZE THE SORE THUMB

The first step to a successful mailbox garden is to soften the junction where the post enters the ground. This calls for compact plants with long seasons of interest. Mounding plants with ornamental evergreen foliage—such as perennials like bergenia (*Bergenia* spp. and cvs., USDA Hardiness Zones 3–9), semishrubs like lavender (*Lavandula* spp. and cvs., Zones 5–9), or cold-hardy shrubs like dwarf conifers—fit the bill perfectly.

Planning from the post out is a good way to ensure that the mailbox blends into the plantings and doesn't stick out like a sore thumb. Match the dimensions of the planting bed to the height of the mailbox so that it feels at home in its setting. As a basic rule, imagine the mailbox tipped over and lying on the ground; if it would remain within the boundaries of the bed, then the bed is large enough.

Match the dimensions of the planting bed to the height of the mailbox.

Arrange the plants around the post so that the post blends into the landscape, balancing the plants' size to the size of bed. But be sure the plants don't obstruct the opening or make it difficult to reach inside the box.

Complement the height of the mailbox by adding a vertical element.

DIVERSIFY HEIGHT AND TEXTURE

Include a complementary vertical element to counterbalance the height of the mailbox and post. Something as simple as a clump of Siberian iris (*Iris* cvs., Zones 3–9) or blue oat grass (*Helictotrichon sempervirens*, Zones 4–9) will do the trick. Be sure to layer your plantings around the post, massing plants with different textures and diverse forms for eye-catching appeal. Select plants that range in color, texture, and size, but avoid thorny or prickly plants.

DECORATE THE POST WITH CLIMBERS

Small annual climbers, such as morning glories (*Ipomoea tricolor* cvs.) and sweet peas (*Lathyrus odoratus* cvs.), will soften the structure of the mailbox post without obscuring it.

Compact perennial vines are not common, but there are a few long-lived options to choose from. Most clematis (*Clematis* spp. and cvs., Zones 4–11) grow too large for the average mailbox, but some new cultivars grow no more than 3 feet to 4 feet tall each season and are covered with large flowers from early summer until late autumn. Climbing miniature roses are also great for mailbox posts. 'Sweet Chariot' (*Rosa* 'Sweet Chariot', Zones 5–10) is a variety that flowers from May until the first frost and is nearly thornless, an important consideration if you want to remain on friendly terms with your postal carrier.

Add pizzazz to your post by planting a vine.

3

BORDERS

Plants with form and texture make
this scene pop. Plants of note include
(clockwise from top): euphorbia
(*Eurphorbia wallichii*, Zones 6–9),
catmint (*Nepeta × faassenii* 'Drop-
more,' Zones 4–8), lady's mantle
(*Alche-milla mollis*, Zones 4–7), and
feather grass (*Stipa tenuissima*,
Zones 7–10).

A NO-NONSENSE APPROACH
TO DESIGN

Beautiful photographs of colorful gardens are inspiring, but designing your garden as an exact replica means you miss the importance of texture and form. Garden designer Amy Fahmy concentrates on filling her garden with plants she loves that will thrive in her yard, and her plan will work for you too.

PERENNIAL BORDERS ARE AN EXCELLENT PLACE TO LEARN FROM failure. If I started where most people start—with the gardening books, magazines, and catalogs—I would do this: Choose my site carefully, decide on a style, and limit my color palette. I would also work with texture and form, use repetition, choose my primary season of bloom, and pick plants for foliage quality. Voilà! The design would then be complete. If it were truly this easy, I would see many more successful gardens than I do. Although all of these elements are important, I don't believe the best borders evolve from this sequence.

Many people think they should sit down with magazines, books, and catalogs as a way to come up with a complete plan for a border. The first thing I notice about borders designed using this method is that color is nearly always carefully coordinated while texture and form are practically ignored. Yet texture and form are far more influential in the border than flower color because they play an ongoing rather than a transitory role. In fact, I've seen

Texture makes color more interesting. The fuzzy leaves of *Stachys byzantina* 'Countess Helen von Stein' (left) and the plumelike inflorescences of *Pennisetum setaceum* 'Rubrum' (below) are their attraction.

some awesome borders that were based solely on form and texture, whereas I have never seen a great border based solely on color.

If you've planned a border based on photographs and it didn't live up to your expectations, your plant choices may have been influenced by the seductive colors in the images. Plants seen through a photographer's lens may look different in a garden. Texture and form are three-dimensional characteristics that often can't compete with colorful blooms in the flat dimensions of a picture. That's why it's often easier to get a sense of the textures and forms of plants by seeing them firsthand.

START WITH PLANTS THAT INSPIRE YOU

My first suggestion is to visit local nurseries and find plants that inspire you. These choices will suggest a complementary or contrasting companion to enrich the border. If you select a bold-textured plant, this may initiate a search for fine-textured plants to accompany it. Choices are more easily made when the available pool of candidates is reduced. A squat, woolly, silver-foliaged plant like *Salvia argentea* (USDA Hardiness Zones 5–8) might call for the delicate airy blooms of *Gaura lindheimeri* 'Siskiyou Pink' (Zones 6–9) to dance above it. The combination of brilliant gold foliage and purple blooms

One plant leads to another. If you are inspired by the bold texture of coneflowers, that can lead you to, say, the fine texture of a sedum. The combination of these two plants will lead you to another, until a border is born.

found in *Tradescantia × andersoniana* 'Sweet Kate' (Zones 5–9) could inspire an entire border of purple and gold.

For years now, I have had a vision of a border that began with the velvety brown bloom of the bearded Iris 'Buffer Zone' (Zones 3–9). Since then, browns, coppers, rusts, and burnished golds have leaped from garden visits into my plans for a brown and gold border, backlit by the western sun. Over time, I've let the salmon-colored *Hedychium coccineum* var. *aurantiacum* 'Flaming Torch' (Zones 7–10) and *Lobelia cardinalis* 'Shrimp Salad' (Zones 3–9) creep in. Thus one plant that caught my attention has suggested an entire border.

KNOW THE VARIATIONS OF A PLANT

My next suggestion comes from observing the talents of several excellent border designers: Get to know the variations of a given plant. Suppose you want the spikes of *Kniphofia uvaria* (Zones 6–9) for your border, but their 24-inch height doesn't fit well. You could substitute *Kniphofia uvaria* 'Lola' (Zones 6–9), with spikes 6 feet tall. Or you could opt for the dwarf *Kniphofia* 'Little Candles' (Zones 6–9) at 18 inches high.

As you increase your repertoire of plants, your border choices become more flexible and the ability to find ideal combinations will improve. Before long, when you want

ABOVE If you want red hot pokers at the back of the border, consider *Kniphofia uvaria* 'Lola', which stands 4 feet taller than the species.

BELOW Get the look you want, where you want it. By knowing your plants, it's an easy switch from canna (left) to curcuma (right).

the look of canna foliage (*Canna* spp. and cvs., Zones 8–11) but not its bloom, you'll just switch to queen lilies (*Curcuma* spp. and cvs., Zones 10–11) or ginger lilies (*Hedychium* spp. and cvs., Zones 7–11). A painter knows about paints: which ones run, which dry quickly, and which produce a desired effect. As an artist in the garden, plants are your paint. Expand the choices on your palette.

FIND OUT HOW A PLANT WILL GROW IN YOUR REGION

Another vital factor in designing a beautiful perennial border is to know what your chosen plants will do when they take hold and grow. If you picked *Rudbeckia maxima* (Zones 4–9) from a picture in a garden magazine or bought it as a 1-gallon nursery plant, you could logically conclude that these black-eyed Susans on 7-foot stems could top the back of your late-summer border. What you wouldn't know is that if you live in the Southeast, this Rudbeckia flops with enriched soil and plenty of water. What a disappointment to find the flowers down near the ground, with all the surrounding perennials growing up through the wildly flopping stems.

All is not lost, however. If you look closer, suddenly you'll see that the bluish cast to the black-eyed Susan's foliage looks great with the burgundy *Canna indica* 'Red Stripe' (Zones 8–10). Furthermore, at ground level, the

If you get lemons, make lemonade. When a plant doesn't behave as it should, like this flopping *Rudbeckia maxima*, consider this an opportunity, not a failure.

yellow blooms electrify the *Aster novae-angliae* 'Purple Dome' (Zones 4–8). If a plant fails to perform as you'd hoped, see if you can use it to your advantage.

FORGET THE PLANNING AND JUST START

Here's one final suggestion that could be the key to your success. Start your border before you decide on a style or create a plan. More often than not, a border bogs down in the planning stage and is then abandoned. Just start. You will learn as much from the mistakes of your first effort as you will from hours of reading, sketching, and planning. Most great borders evolve from the process of trial and error. Let everything that worked well the first year stay and then shuffle around or remove the rest. The first year reveals opportunities for improvement to be made during the next planting season. Because it takes a border at least three years to reach its peak display, the process can be slow. Though it sounds more complicated, the no-plan method often leads to a beautiful garden much faster than you'd expect.

Once you've gardened this way for a while, you will see new value in the classic design concepts touted in the books and magazines, such as color harmony, texture contrast, and repetition of form—and combining these techniques in the garden will soon become second nature.

DESIGN A BORDER
WITH STRONG PLANT SHAPES

After 20 years of tweaking, garden expert Sydney Eddison thought she had achieved perennial border perfection, but she realized its beauty was fleeting, lasting only one month. Her design lacked substance, and she shares how geometry helped provide the weight her garden needed.

NINETEEN EIGHTY-SIX WAS A WONDERFUL GARDENING YEAR FOR me in Connecticut. By mid-July, every inch of my perennial border was in bloom, and I was thrilled. It was just what I had been working toward for 20 years—a summer garden absolutely filled with flowers.

For one glorious month, my heart sang. But even as I rejoiced to see so many daylilies and daisies in bloom all at once, I began to realize that there was more to a beautiful garden than masses of flowers. Although the border was a sea of color, it lacked definition. Like the soft prettiness of extreme youth, its charms were fleeting because it had no form or substance.

Looking at the bed with a more critical eye, I could see it needed structure. The overall effect was colorful but flimsy,

BEFORE

AFTER

A variety of shapes can be the spice of a planting. Years ago, the author's long border was awash in color, but it lacked definition. She revamped the border by adding plant shapes that gave it substance and depth.

CONES

EVERGREEN SHRUBS AND DWARF TREES:

- ARBORVITAES
  (*Thuja occidentalis* 'DeGroot's Spire' and 'Smaragd')

- DWARF ALBERTA SPRUCES
  (*Picea glauca* var. *albertiana* 'Conica', 'Gnome', 'Alberta Globe')

- DWARF BLUE SPRUCES
  (*Picea pungens* 'Fat Albert' and 'Glauca Compacta')

- JUNIPERS
  (*Juniperus communis* 'Compressa')

Broad at the base and tapering to a point, cone shapes carry weight in a garden and provide stability.

and there was too much soft, arching daylily foliage. I also noticed that most of the plants were of a similar height. While the sloping site afforded an element of interest, the measured rise from front to back was monotonous (see the photo on p. 125). There were no surprises—no highs or lows or changes in pace. Nor was there enough variety among the flower shapes. They were either flat or trumpet-shaped and all about the same size.

So I began making gradual changes. I started thinking in terms of the underlying shapes of the plants themselves, like cones, mounds, spikes, fountains, mats and globes. I also started to seriously consider how the shapes related to one another. For example, plants that are strongly three-dimensional contrast with soft clouds of bloom, while spiky foliage provides an antidote to an excess of arching foliage.

ADDING WEIGHT TO A GARDEN'S DESIGN

My stirrings of dissatisfaction about the monotony of my perennial border coincided with a new phase in my gardening life. I had recently met a number of younger garden makers in Connecticut, among them Peter Wooster and his gardener, Gary Keim. Quite apart from being enchanted by them both, I was tremendously impressed with the garden they were creating. It had just what mine lacked: a sturdy framework of shrubs and evergreens to support a mind-boggling collection of annuals, perennials, and tender exotics.

When I asked Peter how he went about arranging the plants, he offered the following tip: If all the plants are about the same size, you need something big to hold it all down. You need height in the middle of the bed from evergreens or shrubs. Then, each bed has corners that should be addressed.

I learned from him that weight exists only in the mind and eye of the beholder, but its presence or absence can be the making of a garden. A compact, well-proportioned evergreen shrub anchors the lighter elements in the composition. Solid geometric shapes like cones, globes, and mounds carry weight. Dark foliage seems heavier and more substantial than light foliage, and large leaves seem weightier than small ones, unless the small ones are dense, uniform, and numerous, as in needled evergreens.

ABOVE Use weighty plants to serve as the bookends of a border. A mounding threadleaf Japanese maple (foreground) and a purple smoke bush (background) define the ends of this long border.

RIGHT Mounds carry weight but are softer and lower in profile than globes.

WAYS TO ADD WEIGHT

While our gardens are very different in layout—Peter's is rectilinear; mine flows with the contours of the land—the same principles apply. Inspired by his example, I sacrificed some of my beloved daylilies to a dwarf Alberta spruce (*Picea glauca* var. *albertiana* 'Conica') (see the photo on the facing page). Its short dark green needles packed into a neat cone shape added weight to the border. I also added vertical fountains of tall ornamental grasses and a few bold, high-rise perennials to break up the groups of false sunflowers (*Heliopsis helianthoides*).

One end of the border had long since been "addressed" by the substantial presence of an old threadleaf Japanese maple (*Acer palmatum* var. *dissectum* 'Crimson Queen'). During the growing season, its woody skeleton is covered with a mass of lacy mahogany red foliage. This dark mound completes the border just as a period completes a sentence. At the opposite end, I added another dark mound, a fast-growing purple smoke bush (*Cotinus coggygria* 'Purple Robe') to balance the maple. By cutting

MOUNDS

SHRUBS:

- BOXWOODS
  (*Buxus sempervirens* cvs.)

- THREADLEAF JAPANESE MAPLES
  (*Acer palmatum* var. *dissectum* 'Crimson Queen')

PERENNIALS:

- BOWLES'S GOLDEN SEDGES
  (*Carex elata* 'Aurea')

- FOUNTAIN GRASSES
  (*Pennisetum alopecuroides*)

- JAPANESE FOREST GRASSES
  (*Hakonechloa macra* 'Aureola')

- HOSTAS
  (*Hosta* spp. and cvs.)

- SILVERMOUND ARTEMISIAS
  (*Artemisia schmidtiana*)

Mimic the natural skyline with the placement of plants. One of the author's borders (left) reflects the same natural contours as a landscape scene in Columbia County, New York.

the smoke bush nearly to the ground every spring, the new growth reaches only about 8 feet high instead of 15 feet and retains its color. Now, the two dark-leaved shrubs hold the border within their embrace, like a pair of bookends (see left photo on p. 127).

Although the changes I made were modest, they transformed the garden. It became interesting to look at even when nothing was in bloom. Instead of a boring straight line, it had a horizon with ups and downs—vertical forms and low, crouching forms (see the photo on p. 124). The addition of the grasses and shrubs provided variety in terms of value as well as form. The green-and-white-striped grasses and the variegated leaves of a red-twig dogwood (*Cornus alba* 'Elegantissima') supplied highlights; the red- and purple-leaved shrubs and the Alberta spruce, contrasting dark accents.

INCORPORATING GEOMETRIC FORMS

Meanwhile, the lessons I had learned from Peter's garden were being incorporated into the two new beds I began working on. These beds divide the "civilized" part of the garden from the wilder part and have an opening between them. To address the ends of the beds on either side of the opening, I planted a pair of Alberta spruces and matching clumps of fountain grass (*Pennisetum alopecuroides*) to give them weight. The forms are distinct and highly contrasting—the evergreens solid and pyramidal; the grasses, despite their name, soft and mound shaped.

Lynden Miller, who was an artist long before she became a designer of public gardens, once said, "If you made a brand-new garden and put in a couple of vertical dwarf evergreens and a couple of rounded ones, you'd be halfway there because you'd have given it geometry." The trick is to fathom nature's underlying geometric forms and to deploy them effectively. Form, of course, can mean either the three-dimensional shape—volume—or the two-dimensional outline of a plant. Both come into play in the design of a garden.

What delights the eye about a range of hills or a distant cityscape is the variety of pleasing forms silhouetted against the sky. The same is true in a flower bed. It was the skyline of my garden that improved so much with the addition of shrubs and other tall plants to give it changes in height (see the photos above).

Within a border, shapely perennials like *Sedum* 'Autumn Joy' provide satisfying three-dimensional forms. I sometimes shape others with a bushy habit into globes or mounds. Threadleaf coreopsis (*Coreopsis verticillata* 'Golden Shower') with its forest of stiff, upright stems and fine, dense foliage lends itself to this treatment. So does *Kalimeris integrifolia*. Its woody stems are lavishly clad in small-toothed leaves and covered with little white daisies. Trimmed into a globe in the spring, it holds its shape throughout the season.

ADDING STRONG LINES AS WELL AS FORM

Good design relies on line as well as silhouette and form. Spears of foliage and flower heads that rise like spires provide high points and are useful to contrast with mounds and globes. In my sunny borders, fuzzy wands of pinkish purple gayfeather (*Liatris spicata* 'Kobold') and pudgy spikes of dusty purple *Agastache foeniculum* serve that purpose. In the shade, the tall white flower spikes of *Hosta* 'Royal Standard' are attractive, rising out of their mounds of lush foliage, with airy white wands of snakeroot (*Actaea racemosa*) waving overhead (see the photo below).

Besides being valuable for their height, tall linear plants like the snakeroot contribute grace and elegance to a flower bed. And the clean lines of yuccas, irises, and certain upright grasses offer refreshing relief from arching foliage or too many plants with a billowing habit.

Hedgehog agave (*Agave stricta*)

Spear-like foliage and spirelike flowers lift the eye skyward.

✳ SPIKES ✳

PERENNIAL FOLIAGE

- BLUE OAT GRASSES
  (*Helictotrichon sempervirens*)

- FEATHER REED GRASSES
  (*Calamagrostis* × *acutiflora* 'Stricta')

- HEDGEHOG AGAVES
  (*Agavae stricta*)

- IRISES
  (*Iris* spp. and cvs.)

- YUCCAS
  (*Yucca filamentosa* cvs.)

PERENNIAL BLOOMS

- BLAZING STARS
  (*Liatris* spp. and cvs.)

- LIGULARIAS
  (*Ligularia stenocephala* 'The Rocket')

- LUPINES
  (*Lupinus* cvs.)

- RED HOT POKERS
  (*Kniphofia* cvs.)

- SNAKEROOTS
  (*Actaea racemosa*)

- SPEEDWELLS
  (*Veronica* spp. and cvs.)

Tall plants that are relatively narrow at the base and flare outward at their tops add grace and elegance to the garden.

Mat-forming plants lie low and tie a garden to its site.

FOUNTAINS

PERENNIALS

- ORNAMENTAL GRASSES
  (*Miscanthus sinensis* 'Variegatus', 'Morning Light', 'Silver Arrow', 'Purpurescens', 'Gracillimus', and 'Zebrinus')

- TALL DAYLILIES
  (*Hemerocallis altissima* 'Statuesque', 'Autumn Minaret', and 'Challenger')

MATS

EVERGREEN SHRUBS:

- LOW, SPREADING JUNIPERS
  (*Juniperus squamata* 'Blue Star'; *J. horizontalis* 'Wiltonii')

PERENNIALS:

- CANDYTUFTS
  (*Iberis sempervirens*)

- LAMBS' EARS
  (*Stachys byzantina*)

- LAMIUNMS
  (*Lamium maculatum* 'White Nancy', 'Beacon Silver', 'Aureum'; and *L. maculatum* f. *album*)

- CREEPING JENNYS
  (*Lysimachia nummularia* 'Aurea')

- THYMES
  (*Thymus* spp. and cvs.)

In the winter, line is the name of the game. At this time of year, I really appreciate ornamental grasses (see the left photo on the facing page). Unless a torrential rain fells them first, *Miscanthus sinensis* 'Morning Light', maiden grass (*M. sinensis* 'Gracillimus'), zebra grass (*M. sinensis* 'Zebrinus'), switch grass (*Panicum virgatum*), and blue oat grass (*Helictotrichon sempervirens*) all stand up to be counted in the winter. But the queen of the border in winter is the threadleaf Japanese maple. Bare, her beautiful zigzag branches cast interesting shadows; trimmed with ridges of snow, they are breathtaking.

The evergreens, of course, come into their own at this time of year. The same Alberta spruces that steadied the flower beds in summer are the stars of the winter border. Solid and reassuring, they stand sentinel at each end of the new beds. The nearby grasses provide a contrast in form and color. In one bed, a globe of variegated boxwood and a neat, twiggy ball of barberry (*Berberis thunbergii* 'Golden Nugget') furnish the edge. A smooth stone, unearthed when I dug the bed, brings the number of rounded forms to three.

This year there will be two new boxwood globes, very small but not to be dismissed. One day, they will take their places at each end of the matching borders with the Alberta spruces and mounds of fountain grass in a trio of satisfying shapes.

Allium giganteum

Globes contrast well with spikes and fountains. Shrubs that do not grow naturally into globes can be pruned into this shape.

GLOBES

DECIDUOUS SHRUBS

- BARBERRIES
  (*Berberis thunbergii* cvs.)

- SPIRAEAS
  (*Spiraea japonica* 'Anthony Waterer' and 'Little Princess')

EVERGREEN SHRUBS

- ARBORVITAES
  (*Thuja occidentalis* cvs.)

- BOXWOODS
  (*Buxus microphylla* 'Winter Gem' and 'Wintergreen'; *B. sempervirens* 'Variegata' and 'Suffruticosa')

- HOLLIES
  (*Ilex glabra* 'Compacta')

PERENNIAL BLOOMS

- ALLIUMS
  (*Allium giganteum*)

- GLOBE THISTLES
  (*Echinops* spp. and cvs.)

A border isn't boring, at least not when you use all of your options. With the right techniques, you can mix subtle and bold plants, formal and informal elements, and attractive structures and hardscape.

✓ **DESIGN IDEAS**
✓ **HARDSCAPES**
✓ **PLANT SUGGESTIONS**

※

THE
LONG BORDER

Garden columnist Jimmy Williams creates a lively, English garden–inspired border at his Tennessee home by using three techniques that defy long border monotony. You can use them on a long border or re-create them on a shorter one.

GERTRUDE JEKYLL, THE DOYENNE OF EARLY-20TH-CENTURY British gardening and mother of the modern mixed border, was ever the optimist. On at least one occasion in her later years, however, she admitted that building a garden takes up about a third of one's time on earth—in learning and putting that knowledge into practice.

After a third of a century of creating, tweaking, and fine tuning, my garden of mixed borders is no exception. It continues to evolve and change. One of the biggest changes occurred after a trip to England to visit Great Dixter, the world-class garden and manor house of Christopher Lloyd, built in 1460. After our trip overseas, I announced to my wife, Peggy, that I wanted to tear up our (then) 18-year-old garden and reinvent it to mimic the idyllic English garden feel of Great Dixter.

My own "Tennessee Dixter," a modest emulation of Great Dixter, is still a work in progress. This long border (actually a series of borders) is not only an oasis but also an ever-changing project, which shows that a garden doesn't have to continue to follow one style started years ago. It can—and should—grow

CREATE DIVERSITY WITHOUT DISTRACTION

Whether you're planning a small bed or one big border, start with a strategy. Otherwise, you may end up with a disjointed, visually unappealing series of plants. Incorporate these elements to create unity within an existing border and to maintain cohesiveness through any future additions:

1 GRADUAL TRANSITIONS

This arbor, in combination with the climbing vines, provides a smooth segue from one garden area to another.

2 DISTINCT AREAS WITHIN THE BORDER

A formal evergreen container, surrounded by a large grouping of pink phlox constitutes a distinct area within this lengthy stretch of border.

3 REPETITION OF KEY ELEMENTS

The pink of the phlox appears throughout the border in the same or similar plants, leading the eye effortlessly along.

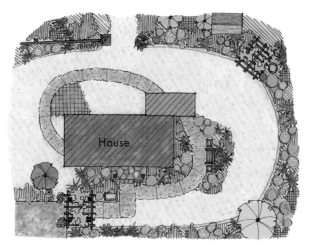

Border length: 380 ft.

and evolve with you. I use three points to build and maintain continuity and beauty in my ever-changing long border: distinct areas within each border, repetition of key elements, and gradual transitions between borders.

DEFY MONOTONY BY CREATING DISTINCT AREAS

When designing a border garden—whether you complete it in one fell swoop or, like I have, take years to add and re-create sections of border—it is important to establish distinct areas within each section to give it life. Diversity,

A good border makes everything better. This strip of lawn becomes a pleasant pathway for the feet, while the eye is admiringly engaged with the garden view.

of course, can easily lead to distraction when there is too much of it. The plant collector's mania always fights with the designer's restraint, with the plant collector often winning. It's all about establishing balance.

Many of the British and other European gardens that I admire are planted exuberantly with masses of informal flowers within formal frameworks, but because the beginnings of my garden were started with informality, I reversed this theme to incorporate distinct formal areas within an informal layout. I establish these formal areas by mixing in yews, box hedges, and stone walls. Pruned into balls, cones, or clouds, boxwoods prove to be valuable

in winter when most perennials dissipate. After leaf fall, the boxwoods seem to jump out of their surroundings. Distinct formal areas are also established by the inclusion of urns, large pots, and topiaries. On the face of it, this reversal to formal within informal, rather than vice versa, would seem incoherent. However, it works surprisingly well.

Large groupings of the same or similar plants also create distinct areas that defy monotony. I depend on summer phloxes, for instance, to pull this off during their season. Big groups of phloxes of the same color dominate in July and August, but they do not overwhelm

Evergreens can be fun and functional. Mix them into your borders to provide repetition and winter interest throughout the border, but avoid monotony by using a variety of shapes.

because, nearby, there is such a plethora of foliage and other colors.

The parts of the border, however, should always be in direct relation to the whole. One way I attempt to avoid the perception of "too much" is to leave a couple of areas in the front of borders for annuals. These are always in one color per location, and the color is one that will blend with perennials of the season. I follow cool-season annuals (violas, pansies, and dianthus) with summer annuals (impatiens, vinca, and wax begonias). These annual plantings produce an effect almost year-round.

CREATE UNITY WITH REPETITION

Repetition within a border establishes continuity, which is an essential part of every garden. It leads the eye, drawing you seamlessly from one section of border to the next. When done well, you barely notice that it's happening.

An easy way to establish repetition is through plant selection. I am enamored with large, bold plants in my borders, and use numerous cannas (*Canna* spp. and cvs., USDA Hardiness Zones 8–11), large coleus (*Solenostemon scutellarioides* cvs., Zone 11), hostas (*Hosta* spp. and cvs., Zones 3–9), and hardy begonias (*Begonia grandis* ssp. *evansiana*, Zones 6–9).

The key to successful repetition with plants is to remember that repeating something doesn't mean that each feature is identical. I use cannas, for instance, in my borders to provide a contrast to fine-foliage plants. But the cannas are different varieties, heights, and leaf shapes. They constitute repetition but not to the point of boredom.

LENGTHEN YOUR GARDEN'S PERFORMANCE

I am disappointed if I do not get at least 10 months of attractiveness from most of my mixed borders. I usually pull this off by following a few simple steps.

DON'T SKIMP ON BULBS AND BLOOMS

If you do some research and planning to get the timing right, you can have blooms from late winter right into summer. Most years, I have hundreds of crocuses, early daffodils, and snowdrops on the move by the end of January.

USE EVERGREENS TO EXTEND THE SEASON

Spring and summer are a garden's prime time, but shrubs and small trees keep the border going late into the gardening season. Many ornamental grasses also last well into winter, carrying on until after Christmas in our climate.

PUT IN SOME HOURS

Regular deadheading and trimming are a prerequisite to season-long appearance—this garden is no low-maintenance wonder. I will even pull some midsummer derelict that has decided to decline and plop in a stop-gap annual or shrub.

And, no, the repetition does not have to be of bold plants, either; simple plants can be just as effective. I use liriope (*Liriope* spp. and cvs., Zones 6–10) in my rock-wall border but in a variety of group sizes and mixed colors.

Color is a great means of repetition, and my borders are all color coded to a certain extent. Most of them are pastel, possibly due to reading too much British-gardening literature. Pastels in the southern United States do have a tendency to wash out, though, which explains why I started a red border in the 1990s. I pull off this bold move from pastels to bright reds using transitional elements.

FUSE BORDERS USING GRADUAL TRANSITIONS

Once repetition is established, it's important in borders like mine—where the long border is actually numerous small gardens joined together—to create a gradual transition from one section of border to another. For gradual transitions, I have found that one of the best ways to blend one group of more prominent perennials with another is with the use of climbers or other plants that weave among their neighbors.

I especially like using perennial geraniums, my favorite among them being hardy geranium (*Geranium sanguineum* var. *striatum*, Zones 3–8). These geraniums, standing alone, will top out at 8 inches but easily climb to 18 inches

LEFT A red border is a bold statement, but there's no reason it has to stand out like a sore thumb. Containers, an open grass pathway, and some stone pillars help make this unique bed a part of the whole.

ABOVE Vines entwine different sections. By climbing up and over this arbor, the vines provide continuity for both sides of the border.

when combined with and allowed to grow into neighboring perennials or shrubs.

My borders also have distinct dividing points that help provide a transition from one section of border to the next, though these are minimal. One border is broken from another, for instance, by a cross path and an arbor with climbing vines. Another arbor joins two other sections of border. Similar colors at adjoining ends of borders soften any change and keep the transition from being too abrupt.

There is one exception to these examples: A 12-foot-wide swath of lawn separates a shaded section of pastels (mostly self-seeded impatiens in summer and fall) and the red border in full sun. In this case, the transition is more

dramatic, and I will say, in all modesty, that some visitors have audibly gasped when turning suddenly from the soft shade colors to the brilliant reds and oranges in full sun. Even here, however, continuity is achieved by using stone mowing strips, pillars, and matching containers to provide a transition from the final pastel border to this hot-colored section of border.

In the grand scheme of things, a third of a century isn't a long time to create and work with a garden you love. With a little know-how, you can easily continue to change and expand your garden year after year. Don't be daunted by the fact that it might take years to build. Start planting. After all, once you start, at least there will be something there the next day.

✳

GOOD LOOKS
BEGIN AT THE EDGE

Tidy, self-supporting plants create the perfect edge in perennial borders. Garden expert Sydney Eddison helps you choose ones that behave well and last all season.

IT MAY BE A SMALL CONTRIBUTION TO ORNAMENTAL horticulture, but I have a theory that if the edges of your perennial borders are crisp and attractive, you are well on the way to a satisfying garden. Well-clad edges create a favorable first impression, reassure garden viewers that all is right with the world, and hide a multitude of sins by diverting attention from weeds or other flaws in the background.

Think of edges as lines that delineate shapes and, at the same time, define adjoining spaces. The edge that contains a flower bed also outlines the shape of the adjacent lawn, path, or ground cover, like the dividing line in the yin-and-yang symbol. Edges create order. They set apart the man-made from the wild and divide space within a garden. They also frame pictures, direct the eye, and provide unity. From a design point of view, they even determine style. Rectilinear edges bespeak formality; curving edges, informality.

The key to an effective edge for your perennial border is suitable plant material. To trace a clear-cut line, you need a tidy, good-looking, self-supporting plant that is highly tolerant of local climatic conditions. Finding perennials that fulfill the obligations of an edging plant is a challenge. Because so much is expected of

Out front, reliable foliage is better than fleeting flowers.

Sedum 'Autumn Joy' nicely finishes the edge of a big border.

REPETITION ALWAYS WORKS WITH EDGERS

Try planting a solid band of a single kind of plant if you have a long, informal, perennial border with curving lines. The uniform edge will give your bed definition and continuity. I edge many beds with a wavy band of lamb's ears. For a long, straight border, several kinds of plants can be united by one theme such as color, shape, or texture. You could make a nice silver edge with *Artemisia stelleriana* 'Silver Brocade', *Veronica incana*, and *Achillea tomentosa*. Or you can easily create unity by repeating groups of a few choice subjects along the front of a bed. The eye delights in recognition, and eagerly leaps from one familiar plant grouping to the next.

them, their numbers are limited, and you have to experiment. You don't really know a plant until you grow it for a few seasons and see how it performs. But to get you started, I've put together a sampler of appealing, well-behaved edgers for a variety of situations.

CHOOSE RELIABLE PLANTS

You need a plant that will emerge from winter dormancy with vigor and mature relatively quickly. A slow developer will leave a gap and interrupt the line of the bed. Most important of all, edgers must have decorative, disease-free, and insect-resistant foliage that retains its color and carriage throughout the growing season.

The foliage requirement is a tall order for flowering plants, which usually go through an ugly phase. Take bearded irises: so handsome in May with their swordlike leaves, so miserable in July when borers leave their blades in tatters. After flowering, even stalwart daylilies lose their charm as the leaves turn yellow. In the middle of a large, mixed border, foliage defects may go unnoticed, but up front and center, they show. For this reason, foliage plants star as edgers. And those with colored leaves really give flowering plants a run for their money.

However, if you are content only with flowers, select those that have comparatively good foliage and boast either a long season of bloom or repeated periods of bloom. Remember that the flowers must not disfigure the plant in their passing, and if shearing after bloom is necessary, select a plant that covers the evidence with new growth.

Height and size are the final considerations in selecting edgers. Keep in mind the dimensions of the bed and the scale of the garden as a whole. My perennial border is 100 feet long and 12 feet to 15 feet wide. It is viewed from a distance and demands big plants to fit into its setting of woodland and overgrown cow pasture. I use 2-foot-tall *Sedum* 'Autumn Joy' as an edger because it is in proportion with the rest of the plants and with the background (see the photo on the facing page). It also measures up in terms of all-season demeanor and excellent foliage. However, a lower-growing sedum such as 'Ruby Glow' would be more suitable for a smaller garden.

SILVERY LAMB'S EARS ARE HARD TO BEAT

Lamb's ears, or *Stachys byzantina*, is my all-time favorite edging plant (see the photo below). This lovely, mat-forming plant has long, elliptical leaves as white as fleece and thickly covered in silky hairs. My perennial bed, which

Silvery-leaved lamb's ears and yellow 'Moonbeam' coreopsis make good edging plants because they keep their neat appearance over a long season.

lies at the foot of an east-facing slope, is bordered with them. They flow northward in a silver stream below the retaining wall, curving gently in and out as the border follows the contours of the hillside. They tie the garden together and look bright and beautiful for eight months of the year, longer in a dry, snowless winter. For a brief period in early spring, the previous year's foliage looks awful, but a vigorous raking clears away the rotted leaves and gives new ones a chance to fill in the gaps.

In most gardening books, the flowers of lamb's ears are criticized for their magenta color and small size. Indeed, they are tiny and deeply imbedded in the thick silver-white fuzz that clothes the 12-inch to 18-inch flower stalks, but I like them. For a couple of weeks, they give the flat ribbon outlining the border another dimension. If you don't want flowers, there is a sterile cultivar called 'Silver Carpet', which is something of a misnomer because the leaves are more gray-green than silver. The large-leaved 'Countess Helen von Stein', which is very bold and handsome, also has gray-green foliage (see the photo below).

Lamb's ears spreads rapidly and self-sows where it is happy. While it prefers full sun, it will grow in partial shade. Its only strict requirement is good drainage. It will rot in standing water and resents high humidity. Otherwise, it is everything an edger should be: easy to grow, tolerant of some extremes in temperature (USDA Hardiness Zones 4–8), and presentable over the long haul.

YEAR-ROUND FOLIAGE AND FALL BLOOM

Variegated liriope (*Liriope muscari* 'Variegata'), which grows well in Zones 6–10, is my next favorite edging plant. In some respects, liriope is superior to lamb's ears as an edger because it remains good looking nearly all year and grows in sun or shade. Variegated forms bleach out in intense sunlight, but given some afternoon shade, their yellow- and green-striped foliage is beyond compare.

The slightly blunt, arching blades of liriope measure ½ inch wide and make neat, grassy tufts about a foot high. The clumps increase generously but do not spread, and they are easy to divide in spring. The narrow spikes of lavender-blue flowers resemble attenuated grape hyacinths. The flowers in early fall add to this plant's value because most perennials are through blooming by then.

If you don't want flowers, then try the gray-green foliage of 'Countess Helen von Stein' lamb's ears.

ABOVE The tidy, grassy tufts of liriope make it an edging favorite.

RIGHT A midsummer shearing keeps catmint edges fresh and flowering.

OPTIONS FOR SUMMER FLOWERS

I am partial to catmint (*Nepeta* spp. and cvs.) and threadleaf coreopsis (*Coreopsis verticillata* and cvs.) for summer-flowering edgers in beds with full sun. These plants are easy to care for, have worthwhile foliage, and flower over a long period. Most catmints thrive in Zones 3–8, coreopsis in Zones 4–9.

Catmint's small, upright, lavender-blue flower clusters appear with the tulips in early spring and go on unabated until about mid-June. At that time, they begin to sprawl, and I shear them. Within a week or two, new foliage begins to appear, and they bloom again—a less impressive flush in midsummer and then another in the fall. The last hurrah is almost as full and long-lasting as the first. In between, soft mops of gray-green foliage decorate the front of the border.

The coreopsis blooms for so long the first time that it can be forgiven for taking a rest afterward. Hundreds of small, yellow, daisylike flowers completely cover the dense network of dainty stems and leaves. When the blooms are spent, they aren't unattractive. They look like little buttons. Cut the whole plant back by about a third with

scissors when the buttons are more numerous than the flowers. The sheared foliage is neat and unobtrusive.

FOLIAGE THAT THRIVES IN THE SHADE

As our garden boasts 11 mature maple trees and is surrounded by forest, shade is a fact of life. If you have a similar situation, don't be dismayed. The *Hosta* genus

TOP To edge a shady bed, the overlapping leaves of hosta won't disappoint.

ABOVE Combining hostas with flowering perennials can yield a well-behaved bed.

alone offers dozens of small-leaved cultivars to furnish the edge of a woodland path or tree-shaded border. Hosta gets four stars for magnificent foliage, which comes in shades of green, blue, and gold. Hostas thrive in Zones 3–9 and like soil rich in organic matter, although they will make do in average soil.

'Hadspen Blue' and 'Blue Cadet' have wonderful frosty blue-green leaves and form dense, low mounds of overlapping leaves. 'Gold Edger' has heart-shaped,

bright chartreuse to gold leaves and develops into a neat, 10-inch, dome-shaped clump. Nifty little 'Kabitan' has narrow, pointed, yellow leaves with wavy edges trimmed in dark green. 'Golden Tiara' is fast growing to about 1 foot by 16 inches and has small, heart-shaped, or cordate, leaves. Green forms abound, and the species *H. tardiflora* is one of the best with very dark green leaves.

Generally, the white or lavender flowers of hostas are disappointing in appearance, though often sweetly scented. The spikes of drooping bells start to bloom from the bottom up, and the spent blossoms detract from those that are opening. However, some cultivars have better flowers than others. Those of *H. tardiflora* are exceptional. The spikes are crowded with lavender bells and are very decorative.

EDGERS FOR SHADY BEDS

As neat edgers for shady areas, epimediums run hostas a close second. These deceptively delicate-looking plants tolerate dry shade with equanimity and provide charming spring flowers, as well as lovely foliage. Before the leaves unfurl, thin stems arise, carrying airy sprays of spidery blossoms in rose-pink, yellow, or white. In mild climates, epimediums keep their leaves almost all winter. They grow in Zones 4–8.

Epimedium grandiflorum has two popular cultivars, both desirable: 'Rose Queen' and 'White Queen'. The species

SOLUTIONS FOR MOIST SOIL

Lady's mantle (*Alchemilla mollis*), hardy from Zones 4–7, is a beautiful edger for rich, moist soil and partial shade. Although it tends to look shabby in my dry perennial border, it thrives in my friend Martha McKeon's border and looks lovely combined with hostas. The silvery, sea green leaves are palmate and precisely pleated. In the morning they catch the dew, each one supporting a tiny crystal ball. Frothy, chartreuse flowers are an added attraction in early summer. Cut the flowers and leaves down when they begin to look messy. New foliage will soon fill in.

Heucheras (*Heuchera* spp. and cvs.) are another of Martha's most successful edging plants. They grow happily in either full sun or part shade, but they need moisture-retentive soil to perform well. In suitable soil, heucheras favor the gardener with masses of tiny, bell-shaped flowers in loose sprays at the top of fine, but sturdy, 2-foot stalks. These stand above neat clumps of rounded, scalloped leaves. The flower colors run the gamut of pinks, reds, and white, with many named cultivars.

Today, new selections are being made with the emphasis on foliage. *Heuchera* 'Montrose Ruby' has

Heuchera's rounded or scalloped leaves are perfect for a moist edge.

stunning, dark-red foliage; 'Pewter Veil' is a knockout with silver-frosted red leaves; and *H. micrantha* 'Palace Purple' is deservedly popular for its rich red-purple leaves. All the heucheras are well-behaved edgers and grow in Zones 4–8.

E. × rubrum has crimson flowers, and a cultivar of *E. × versicolor* called 'Sulphureum' comes in yellow. While the flowers are delightful close up, they are not showy, except en masse. However, the foliage that follows is outstanding for its elegance. Branched stems displaying angel-wing leaflets form graceful mounds. *E. × rubrum* has particularly fetching leaves, red-veined and often flushed with red at the edges. In the fall, they assume shades of red and bronze, and cling to the stems until December.

Without knowing anything about it, I once bought a tiny pot of *Vancouveria hexandra* from a North American Rock Garden Society plant sale. I have since come to delight in this graceful cousin of epimedium as a lacy edging for large-leaved hostas. The white flowers of vancouveria are so minute that they really don't count, although if you examine them carefully, their shape is intriguing. They are called "inside-out flowers" for their reflexed sepals, which look as if the wind had blown them backward.

Delicate, compound foliage is vancouveria's greatest asset. The individual leaflets are small, rounded, or lobed, and about ¾ inch across on wiry, threadlike stems. Indigenous to the moist woods of the Pacific Northwest, this engaging plant is surprisingly tolerant of dry shade and hardy as well.

TIPS FOR DRIVEWAY STRIPS

It's not easy to design plantings for a 2-foot-wide scrap of land between the driveway and the front walk or the edge of your property. Faced with limited growing space, trauma from automobile and pedestrian traffic, and the effects of pollutants, driveway strips pose a significant design challenge for many urban and suburban gardeners. The keys to a successful driveway strip are making it seem less skinny than it is and ensuring that it looks like a part of the overall landscape, not just an afterthought. The strategic use of plants and some clever construction details can transform this forlorn nuisance area into a healthy and attractive landscape asset that adds curb appeal to your property.

MAKE A NARROW AREA SEEM WIDER

To deemphasize its narrowness and length, a driveway strip should be planted in diagonal drifts that lead your eyes to zigzag back and forth, slowing their journey down the length of the strip. If you toss in a variety of plant forms, textures, and colors, the planting strip will look like a legitimate border, not an afterthought.

Punctuate low plantings using accent plants with an upright habit to break up the strip into segments and further deemphasize its length. Upright plants are even more effective if they're spaced irregularly so that the eyes don't trip past them too quickly. Echoing the driveway-strip plantings elsewhere in the yard integrates the driveway with the rest of the landscape.

A Group plants in drifts to deemphasize the narrowness of the bed.

B Use upright plants to break up the length of the strip.

C Use compact plants to keep the driveway and walkway clear.

D Echo plantings elsewhere in the yard for visual continuity.

A Keep tall plants away from the street to ensure good visibility.

B Vary plant heights to create an illusion of depth.

C Use an assortment of forms, textures, and colors to keep things looking lively.

D Rely on compact climbers to break up horizontal lines.

CLIMBING PLANTS HELP ALONG A PROPERTY LINE

Designing for a narrow strip between your driveway and the property line poses unique challenges. Often, a fence divides one property from another, making the narrow strip appear even skinnier. Interrupt the long line of the fence's top rail to dissolve this unfortunate illusion. Climbing plants that clamber over the top of a fence serve this function especially well. I recommend compact clematis (*Clematis* spp. and cvs., USDA Hardiness Zones 4–11) and climbing roses (*Rosa* spp. and cvs., Zones 2–11) because these plants won't damage the fence the way heavier climbers, like wisteria or Boston ivy, can.

Planted as lawn, driveway strips are inconvenient to mow and require lots of water with overhead irrigation, which can put more water on the pavement than on the lawn. Choose drought-tolerant shrubs and perennials instead, but when selecting plants, pay close attention to their mature sizes. Narrow plants that won't grow into the walk or driveway are best. Avoid setting tall plants too close to the street end of a driveway strip because they're liable to block views of oncoming traffic.

DROUGHT- AND SALT-TOLERANT PLANTS

Narrow strips along a driveway often prove challenging to many plants. The following 15 plants require little irrigation, can take the reflective heat close to paved surfaces, and survive harsh pollutants from the street and driveway.

Bearberry
(*Arctostaphyllos uva-ursi* and cvs., Zones 2–6)

Blue-mist shrub
(*Caryopteris × clandonensis* cvs., Zones 6–9)

Cinquefoil
(*Potentilla* spp. and cvs., Zones 3–8)

Cotoneaster
(*Cotoneaster* spp. and cvs., Zones 4–8)

Euphorbia
(*Euphorbia* spp. and cvs., Zones 4–11)

Heath and heather
(*Erica* spp. and cvs., Zones 5–11)

'Karl Foerster' feather reed grass
(*Calamagrostis × acutiflora* 'Karl Foerster', Zones 5–9)

Lavender
(*Lavandula* spp. and cvs., Zones 5–9)

Lilyturf
(*Liriope muscari* and cvs., Zones 6–10)

Phormium
(*Phormium* spp. and cvs., Zones 8–11)

Rosemary
(*Rosmarinus officinalis* and cvs., Zones 8–11)

Sea holly
(*Eryngium* spp. and cvs., Zones 3–11)

Sedum
(*Sedum* spp. and cvs., Zones 3–9)

St. John's wort
(*Hypericum* spp. and cvs., Zones 5–9)

Statice
(*Limonium* spp. and cvs., Zones 7–9)

Hardworking perennials—such as fountain grass, with its wispy flower heads—help create the backbone of a mixed border.

THE BEST PLANTS FOR
SUNNY BORDERS

Everyone wants beautiful flowers in their garden, but reliability matters too when choosing plants. Garden expert Sydney Eddison suggests workhorse perennials for the border that last throughout the seasons.

IN MY DAY, FARMERS VALUED WORKHORSES FOR THEIR STRONG constitutions, good manners, and steady dependability. As a gardener, I appreciate these same qualities in a handful of sun-loving perennials that earn their keep day in, day out, year after year.

These plants contribute to the garden from the time they appear in the spring until the end of the growing season and, in some cases, beyond. Each has been in my garden for five years or longer.

None of my eight workhorses requires frequent division, but all welcome it and will provide plenty of extra plants. With the exception of the grasses, all can be divided when it's convenient, in either spring or fall. Grasses don't take kindly to being disturbed in the fall, so divide them only in the spring. Because grasses have deep roots, it's hard work, so do it sooner rather than later.

Although I improve my clay soil with a yearly mulch of chopped leaves in the spring and add compost to each planting hole, my soil falls short of the ideal of rich loam. Nonetheless, these plants are robust and happy. They are likely to thrive in most garden soils. Include workhorse plants in your border, and you'll have time to fuss with your more temperamental treasures.

broad, short rays with pinked edges encircle a little knob of disk flowers. In my sloping, not-quite-sunny-enough border, I have to put a girdle of stakes and string around the stems, but on level ground and in full sun, this chore would not be necessary.

PERSIAN CATMINT REBLOOMS AFTER IT'S SHEARED

Persian catmint (*Nepeta racemosa*, Zones 4–8), which has been growing in my garden for more than 30 years, was the gift of my gardening mentors, Helen and John Gill. It begins to bloom at the same time as Darwin tulips and keeps going through peony season, sending up innumerable racemes of little violet-blue flowers above a mound of gray-green leaves. The first flush lasts until mid-June, at which point the mound becomes loose and floppy. Shearing with a pair of garden scissors quickly restores order; before long, fresh, leafy stems arise to cover the damage and send up new flower stalks. Intermittent bloom throughout the summer is followed by another substantial flowering in late September. At

'BUTTERPAT' SNEEZEWEED BEARS BRIGHT YELLOW BLOOMS

Rudely and unfairly called sneezeweed, *Helenium* 'Butterpat' (USDA Hardiness Zones 4–8) makes the grade for its masses of sunny, yellow flowers in August and September. Other species and cultivars of Helenium come in russet red and in orange, but yellow is my favorite. In the middle to the back of the border, the leafy 4-foot- to 5-foot-tall stems of 'Butterpat' support large, loose terminal clusters of 2-inch, daisylike flowers, whose

RIGHT 'Zagreb' tickseed

LEFT Variegated lilyturf
in autumn

BELOW Variegated lilyturf

the front of the border, Persian catmint can be relied on to look attractive for most of the growing season. While I have grown several species and cultivars of *Nepeta* and enjoyed them all, Persian catmint remains a sentimental favorite.

'ZAGREB' IS A STURDY TICKSEED

Several North American tickseeds (*Coreopsis* spp. and cvs.) have earned their place in gardens, but the thread-leaved tickseed (*C. verticillata*, Zones 4–9) is by far the best. Indeed, the pale yellow cultivar called 'Moonbeam' was once chosen Perennial Plant of the Year™ by the Perennial Plant Association®, but in my garden, the egg-yolk yellow 'Zagreb' has displayed a much sturdier constitution. The dense upright stems, thickly set with fine needlelike leaves, spread steadily by underground stolons into large patches, which need a bit of chopping back in the spring. This, to me, does not constitute an invasion. I have clumps

at intervals all along the front of my borders. I love its neat, shrubby appearance before and after bloom and delight in its abundance of bright yellow flowers starting early in July and persisting for weeks.

VARIEGATED LILYTURF MAKES A PERFECT EDGER

It's easy to sing the praises of variegated lilyturf (*Liriope muscari* 'Variegata', Zones 6–10). Its impeccable green-striped-with-cream foliage is vibrant and grasslike, but the leaves are wider and more blunt at their tip than grasses. Ideal as an edging plant, a clump runs from 1 foot to 1½ feet tall and half again as wide. The crisp, virtually indestructible leaves look attractive all season and often well into the winter. Nor are the spikes of small blue-violet flowers anything to sneeze at (see the top left photo above). They appear in late September—when few flowers are in bloom—and continue through the middle

'Snowbank' boltonia

'Autumn Joy' sedum (early spring)

'Autumn Joy' sedum (late summer)

'Autumn Joy' sedum (early autumn)

of October. Another virtue of variegated lilyturf is its tolerance of shade. Indeed, it bleaches out a bit in full sun, preferring morning sun and afternoon shade, and it will put up with moderate to dense shade as well.

'SNOWBANK' BOLTONIA SHINES IN SEPTEMBER

'Snowbank' boltonia (*Boltonia asteroides* 'Snowbank', Zones 4–9) is a cultivar of a plant native to the eastern and central United States. 'Snowbank' is ideal for the middle of the border and seldom needs staking. The strong, straight, 4-foot-tall stems begin branching partway up and are clad in willowlike blue-green leaves. In fact, the foliage is about as good as it gets and makes a fine background for shorter plants. To top it off, the upper two-thirds of the plant becomes a cloud of white daisy flowers in mid-September.

'AUTUMN JOY' SEDUM CHANGES ITS LOOK WITH THE SEASONS

Beautiful and bulletproof, the chameleon-like nature of *Sedum* 'Autumn Joy' (Zones 3–10) has always appealed to me. Poised for early-spring growth, its small, tight, blue-green rosebuds have already emerged at the base of each stem, sometimes even as the snow flies. By April, the blue-green rosettes have elongated into succulent, leafy stems (see the top right photo on the facing page), which, at the end of May, are tall enough to mask the dying foliage of spring bulbs. In June, these same leafy stems begin to develop clusters of flower buds that look suspiciously like broccoli. In August, the flat flower clusters begin to turn from pale green to pink (see center right on the facing page). At their most colorful—from the end of the month through the middle of September—the flowers of 'Autumn Joy' deepen from pink to rose to russet to brown. Allowed to remain upright, the 2-foot-tall dried stalks and brown heads stand out against the snow.

FOUNTAIN GRASS LASTS ALL YEAR

Fountain grass (*Pennisetum alopecuroides* Zones 6–9) stands out for its excellent habit and stunning year-long beauty (see the photo on p. 150). Given a generous 3-foot to 4-foot circle around each clump, fountain grass develops into a 3-foot-tall, perfectly symmetrical mound of narrow, arching blades, which makes a superb background for my daylilies. Fuzzy mauve flower heads appear in late summer, adding much to the charm of this grass and about a foot to its height. In fall, its leaves turn golden (see the top photo at right) and then gradually fade to tan in winter. Last spring, I divided the two clumps of fountain grass that hold down the ends of matching borders at the far end of my garden. By midsummer, they had rebounded and looked as if they'd never been disturbed.

'MORNING LIGHT' MISCANTHUS GLEAMS IN A BORDER

My other favorite grass is *Miscanthus sinensis* 'Morning Light' (Zones 4–9). It's a huge temptation to add zebra grass (*M. sinensis* 'Zebrinus') and maiden grass (*M. sinensis* 'Gracillimus') to this list; they miss out only because they both require staking. In contrast, 'Morning Light' is self-supporting and arguably the most beautiful. The inner light, which accounts for its name, emanates from the white midribs of its fine-textured leaf blades and the threads of white around their edges. A shimmering miracle of grace between 5 feet and 6 feet tall, 'Morning Light', like fountain grass, turns golden in November and fades to beige in winter.

Fountain grass (autumn)

'Morning Light' miscanthus

The bold, colorful leaves of 'Black Magic' taro make their presence known in this mixed shrub and perennial border.

A BORDER WITH A
TROPICAL PUNCH

Exotic plants can be a life-saver in warmer climates. To give her garden some summer color, writer and tropical plant expert Pam Baggett stopped fighting the heat and embraced tropical plants as a garden mainstay.

I GARDEN IN A STEAM BATH. AT LEAST THAT'S WHAT IT FEELS like by mid-July, when daytime temperatures approach triple digits. Perennials that flower for months in cool climates often wave a flag of surrender to the heat after three weeks in North Carolina, as I learned to my chagrin when I began building large-scale perennial borders 15 years ago. Not wanting my garden to play poor step sister to the exquisite herbaceous borders I'd seen in British garden books, I gradually expanded my plant repertoire over the years to include woody shrubs and summer-flowering bulbs. I created lovely but sedate mixed borders that still, unfortunately, seemed to be lacking in foliar and floral drama, at least once spring's frantic rush of blossoms had faded.

For colorful, lush borders from mid-May to late October's frost, I began looking to the tropics, where daylight hovers around 12 hours all year long and temperatures remain well above freezing. At the equator, tropical perennials provide nonstop blooms and exotically hued foliage year-round. As it turns out, they adapt beautifully to most of the United States, too. They're least happy in the Pacific Northwest and the southwestern desert regions, but I get rave reports from friends and customers from

the rest of the country, from Milwaukee to Miami. Given the excellent health and extended performance of tropicals, I'm willing to grow them as annuals, though quite a few function as perennials in USDA Hardiness Zones 7a and higher.

Regardless of whether I have to replant my favorites every year, I still grow masses of equatorial beauties. Planted in late spring after night temperatures remain above 50°F, tropical plants take off in early summer's heat and grow with vigor until the first fall frost, bridging the gap between June's day lilies and autumn's asters. After years of experimentation, I've developed some useful design strategies for incorporating tropicals into traditional mixed borders.

USE BIG, BOLD LEAVES AS FOCAL POINTS

Ask any garden designer and you will hear that bold, oversize foliage is critical to a dramatic visual picture. The most successful borders that I've seen mix a range of tiny to towering textures to keep plantings of traditional perennials and shrubs from looking too busy. By placing big-leaved tropicals as focal points at intervals along

LEFT Red-leaf Abyssinian banana sets the stage with its strong lines, structure, and rich color.

Bed of nails

Gold-vein plant

Prince's feathers

a border, you can create a visual respite from jumbled masses of undifferentiated, frilly textures, while achieving visual movement through the border. This can be effective right up to the border's front edge, where textures tend to be timid.

Some tropicals produce leaves so large you could wrap yourself up in them. If you live in the extreme northern or northwestern United States, cold-hardy ornamental rhubarbs (*Rheum* spp. and cvs., Zones 5–9) and butterburs (*Petasites* spp. and cvs., Zones 5–9) serve up similarly bold foliage, but in much of the country, these plants collapse from heatstroke in midsummer. Meanwhile, jumbo-leaved

tropicals like banana and butterfly ginger lily thrive under these conditions.

Red-leaf Abyssinian banana makes as bold a statement as a gardener could hope for. Over one summer, it can grow up to 8 feet tall, sporting burgundy-backed leaves 6 feet or longer. It becomes an instant anchor, drawing the eye up and out along the smooth length of its leaves, when nestled in a bed of burgundy prince's feather, hardy golden groundsel (*Ligularia dentata* 'Desdemona', Zones 4–8), golden sunflowers (*Rudbeckia hirta* 'Irish Eyes' and 'Indian Summer', Zones 3–7), and Dahlia 'Bishop of Llandaff' (see the photo on the facing page).

Not every focal point, however, has to be the tallest plant in sight. Grown as an annual, bed of nails only reaches 30 inches to 40 inches tall, but its broad leaves are 24 inches across; they're made even more eye-catching by the inch-long purple thorns protruding from the veins. The little elephant's ear *Colocasia* 'Hilo Beauty' is even shorter—only 2 feet tall—but its cream-spotted leaves

The burgundy and coral stripes of Canna Tropicanna®
pop against deeply colored neighboring plants.

Shisos

Dahlia

Persian shield

grow a foot long, making a wonderful contrast with finer-textured, low-growing plants.

ADD TROPICALS AS ACCENTS

The safest way to experiment with tropicals in the garden is to add them as color accents, inserting a single plant into an open space where its colorful flowers or foliage can add spice all season long. Coordinate the scene by thinking about the flower and foliage colors of surrounding perennials and shrubs. Try selecting a

tropical that will enhance the setting rather than clash with established plantings.

For example, perennial asters earn their keep by providing a great show in autumn, but for several months before bloom time, you're left with a mound of nondescript green foliage. Meanwhile, tropical Persian shield looks like a stained-glass window all season long, featuring metallic purple foliage etched with black-green veins. In sun or shade, the foliage of this 30-inch-tall tropical serves as an outstanding color accent, which you can successfully play against any number of colors from

TROPICAL PLANT CHOICES

PLANT NAME	ZONES
PLANTS FOR FOCAL POINTS	
ANGELS' TRUMPETS (*Brugmansia* spp. and cvs.)	8–10
BED OF NAILS (*Solanum quitoense*)	10–11
BUTTERFLY GINGER LILIES (*Hedychium coronarium*)	9–10
CANNAS (*Canna* cvs.)	7–11
COPPERLEAFS (*Acalypha wilkesiana* and cvs.)	11
ELEPHANT'S EARS (*Alocasia* spp. and cvs.)	11
GOLD-VEIN PLANTS (*Sanchezia speciosa*)	11
HARDY BANANAS (*Musa basjoo*)	8–10
RED BANANAS (*Musa zebrine*)	8–10
RED-LEAF ABYSSINIAN BANANAS (*Ensete ventricosum* 'Maurelii' and cvs.)	10–11
SHELL GINGERS (*Alpinia zerumbet* and cvs.)	8–10
TAROS (*Colocasia* spp. and cvs.)	7–11
PLANTS FOR ACCENTS	
ALTERNAWSAGES (*Salvia* spp. and cvs.)	7–10
CANNAS (*Canna* cvs.)	7–11
CENTAUREAS (*Centaurea gymnocarpa* and cvs.)	7–9
COLEUSES (*Solenostemon scutellarioides* cvs.)	11
CUPHEAS (*Cuphea* spp. and cvs.)	10–11
DAHLIAS (*Dahlia* cvs.)	8–11
FOUNTAIN GRASSES (*Pennisetum setaceum* and cvs.)	9–10
LANTANAS (*Lantana camara* cvs.)	11
PERSIAN SHIELD (*Strobilanthes dyerianus*)	8–11
PIGEON BERRIES (*Duranta erecta* and cvs.)	11
PRINCE'S FEATHERS (*Amaranthus hypochondriacus* cvs.)	11
SHISOS (*Perilla frutescens* and cvs.)	11
STAR CLUSTERS (*Pentas lanceolata* and cvs.)	11
TROPICAL MINTS (*Plectranthus* spp. and cvs.)	11
TROPICAL SMOKE BUSHES (*Euphorbia cotinifolia*)	9–11

Annual sage

silver, chartreuse, or orange to the soft pink flowers of *Sedum telephium* 'Matrona' (Zones 4–9). And when the feathery, royal purple to pale pink blossoms of the asters (*Aster novae-angliae* cvs., Zones 4–8) do appear, the effect is striking against Persian shield's mesmerizing foliage.

Because of their gigantic leaves and outrageous flowers, cannas are typically thought of as focal points, but they make exciting color accents, too. When tucked into a space between wispy perennial grasses, the gold-striped leaves of 6-foot-tall Canna 'Pretoria' make a perfect color echo for low-mounding 'Bowles' Golden' sedge (*Carex elata* 'Bowles' Golden', Zones 5–9). At the same time, the canna's flaming tangerine blossoms strike a fiery note, setting the coppery plumes of late-blooming *Miscanthus sinensis* 'Morning Light' (Zones 4–9) aglow.

CREATE A VIGNETTE

My first tropical vignette came compliments of the local deer, and for once (and only once) I am grateful for their visit. Faced with a midsummer gap and a large group of visitors due in six weeks, I yanked out the grazed stubs of perennials and frantically filled the space with fast-growing tropicals. The plants grew so fast that they filled the space with time to spare, and I was hooked on a new

garden style. Now, my borders always have open coves where tropicals can time-share with fall-planted, spring-blooming bulbs.

For the best results, give your coves sturdy backdrops of robust perennials or shrubs. Select perennials with especially good foliage and that reach as tall as 4 feet or more, like Joe Pye weeds (*Eupatorium* spp. and cvs., Zones 3–9), Culver's root (*Veronicastrum virginicum*, Zones 3–8), ironweed (*Vernonia noveboracensis*, Zones 5–9), swamp sunflower (*Helianthus angustifolius*, Zones 6–9), and ornamental grasses. In choosing companion tropicals, I pay attention to color echo and contrast, and I also make sure to designate a dramatic focal point for each composition.

At almost 7 feet tall, black stem taro (*Colocasia esculenta* 'Fontanesii') can certainly serve as a focal point for a shrub-backed tropical cove. With its somber 3-foot-long leaves, 'Fontanesii' makes a great centerpiece for wine-purple sage (*Salvia vanhouttei* 'Paul', Zones 9–10) and self-seeding annual shiso. Purple leaf sand cherry (*Prunus × cistena*, Zones 4–8) adds another dose of purple to the scene, while woody gold-leaf yellow bells (*Forsythia × intermedia* 'Goldleaf', Zones 6–9) and blue juniper (*Juniperus scopulorum* 'Wichita Blue', Zones 4–7) provide remarkable color contrasts.

Another idea is to anchor a vignette with the grand, gold-ribboned foliage of Peruvian gold-vein plant. Echo its color with variegated pigeon berry. Add wine red coleus 'Oxblood' and red and yellow 'New Hurricane' to accent the ruby stems of gold-vein plant (see the photo on the facing page). Contrast all that flashy brightness with lots of dark foliage, like giant burgundy fountain grass, shrubby purple smoke bush (*Cotinus coggygria* 'Purple Robe', Zones 5–8), and black-leaved 'Bishop of Llandaff' dahlia.

Adding tropical accents, focal points, and coves to my borders has created dimensions of color and texture I only dreamed of when I first began gardening. Best of all, I no longer pine for the British look in my garden beds. I've found my own style, one that works for my climate and tastes, with plants that look super from planting time until fall frost.

1 Gold-vein plant
(*Sanchezia speciosa*, Zone 11)

2 Burgundy fountain grass
(*Pennisetum setaceum* 'Burgundy Giant',
Zones 9–10)

3 Dark red coleus
(*Solenostemon scutellarioides* 'Oxblood',
Zone 11)

4 Variegated pigeon berry
(*Duranta erecta* 'Golden Edge', Zone 11)

5 Red, burgundy, and yellow coleus
(*Solenostemon scutellarioides* 'New
Hurricane', Zone 11)

Create a room with a view. Long-blooming perennials that stand up to sweltering heat look stunning when this patio is used most.

✻

A BORDER
THAT PLEASES ALL SUMMER LONG

Installing a pool in her yard inspired landscape designer Suzanne Knutson to create a summer garden of colorful perennials. And the best part is the flowers and shrubs practically take care of themselves.

WHEN MY HUSBAND AND I MOVED INTO OUR HOUSE, OUR FIRST priority was to put in a pool. With demanding careers that left us precious little time for ourselves, we envisioned a private outdoor oasis where we could relax together at the end of the week. So we made an enclosed backyard space, including the pool, a surrounding patio, and generous garden beds filled with perennials and flowering shrubs. Before we had children, it was our quiet sanctuary, and now it's become a gathering center for our growing family. Whatever the function of a patio used mostly in summer, it's not the place for fussy plantings, which is something I learned the hard way. Once I realized that, I gradually created a garden that enhances our hot-weather leisure activities and requires only minimal maintenance.

1 'Moonshine' yarrow (*Achillea* 'Moonshine')

2 Oriental lily (*Lilium* 'Mona Lisa')

3 Shasta daisy (*Leucanthemum* × *superbum* 'Becky')

4 Hollyhock (*Alcea rosea* 'Old Barnyard Mix')

5 Cheddar pink (*Dianthus gratianopolitanus* 'Firewitch')

6 Perennial salvia (*Salvia* × *sylvestris* 'May Night')

7 'Moonbeam' coreopsis (*Coreopsis* 'Moonbeam')

8 Verbena (*Verbena* × *hybrida* 'Temari Patio Hot Pink')

9 Hollyhock (*Alcea rosea* 'Powderpuff Mix')

10 Daylily (*Hemerocallis* 'Hyperion')

11 Lambs' ears (*Stachys byzantina* 'Countess Helen von Stein')

12 Bee balm (*Monarda didyma* 'Marshall's Delight')

CREATE AN APPEALING VIEW

While our pool was being installed, I turned my attention to the landscape. I pictured a long perennial border running along one side of the pool that would camouflage an obtrusive fence and offer a delightful view that we could enjoy as we swam or relaxed on the patio. Brimming with optimism but with nary a clue about the growth habits and bloom times of the flowers I envisioned for our garden, we dug a bed 8 feet wide and roughly 60 feet long. Then I began the highly enjoyable process of selecting plants for my new perennial garden. It didn't take long, however, before I realized that it takes more than enthusiasm to create a garden that pleases all summer long.

Oh sure, my garden was absolutely delightful the following spring, stuffed as it was with early-blooming perennials such as peonies (*Paeonia* spp. and cvs.), lady's mantle (*Alchemilla mollis*), pinks (*Dianthus* spp. and cvs.), and Siberian irises (*Iris sibirica* and cvs.). Admiring my garden that spring for the umpteenth time, I congratulated myself on what a masterful gardener I had become.

As spring faded into summer, however, and my beautiful garden likewise faded into a distant memory, it dawned on me that there weren't enough remaining perennials to offer interest during the rest of the growing season. Particularly distressing was the fact that in early spring, when my garden was at its peak, it was usually too chilly to spend much time in the pool or on the patio.

PLAN FOR PEAK BLOOM TIMES

Dismayed at the thought of spending the entire summer staring at a garden past its prime, I began to prowl nurseries looking for intriguing plants that were in bloom when I needed them most: in July and August. So I gradually reworked the border to make it more of a summer garden. To be fair, the garden does look showy in spring, but now it's also colorful during the dog days of summer.

Anchoring this garden are large boxwoods and summer-blooming shrubs such as *Hydrangea macrophylla* 'Nikko Blue', rose of Sharon (*Hibiscus syriacus* and cvs.), and *Rosa* 'Bonica'. Around these shrubs I've planted many summer-blooming flowers, including hollyhocks (*Alcea rosea* cvs.), which give the garden instant charm as well as height, and Oriental lilies (*Lilium* cvs.), which take up little room while offering extravagant blooms and intoxicating fragrance. Other strong summer performers are Shasta daisies (*Leucanthemum* × *superbum* cvs.), purple coneflowers (*Echinacea purpurea* 'Magnus'), and low-growing asters (*Aster* spp. and cvs.). Also, by religiously deadheading the spent flower heads of certain perennials, such as foxgloves (*Digitalis purpurea* and cvs.) and 'May Night' sage (*Salvia* × *sylvestris* 'May Night'), I can extend their bloom time through August.

CHOOSE LOW-CARE PLANTS

One of the most enjoyable pursuits my summer garden has afforded me is the chance to tinker with different plants. I've found that flowers with soft pastel shades get completely washed out under the harsh glare of the summer sun. Now, I save most soft-colored flowers for the spring garden, when the sun is lower in the sky and less intense. I rely, instead, on the yolk-colored flowers of black-eyed Susan (*Rudbeckia fulgida* var. *sullivantii* 'Goldsturm'), the vivid pink blooms of garden phlox (*Phlox paniculata* 'Eva Cullum'), and the sulfur yellow blooms of yarrow (*Achillea* 'Moonshine'). Two other favorites that can withstand the sun's intensity are 'Firewitch' pink (*Dianthus gratianopolitanus* 'Firewitch'), which forms a low-growing mat of silvery blue foliage topped by bright magenta flowers, and the easy-care shrub rose called Knock Out®, which lives up to its name.

I've also learned that it's essential to fill a summer garden with low-maintenance plants that have long bloom times and attractive habits (see "Robust Summer Bloomers" on p. 168). Chief among these are 'Moonbeam' coreopsis (*Coreopsis* 'Moonbeam'), several ornamental grasses, black-eyed Susans, late-blooming astilbes, low-growing asters, the ever-reliable *Sedum* 'Autumn Joy', and *Sedum spectabile* 'Brilliant', which is more compact than 'Autumn Joy' and has bright lavender-pink blooms. All these perennials look attractive from the moment they emerge in spring until the first frost in October. Best of all, they require almost no maintenance.

ROBUST SUMMER BLOOMERS

PLANT NAME	ZONES	HEIGHT
SMALL		
'BECKY' SHASTA DAISY (*Leucanthemum × superbum* 'Becky')	5–8	2–3 ft.
BLACK-EYED SUSAN (*Rudbeckia fulgida* var. *sullivantii* 'Goldsturm')	4–9	2–ft.
BLUE MIST SHRUB (*Caryopteris × clandonensis* cvs.)	6–9	2–3 ft.
COREOPSIS (*Coreopsis* 'Moonbeam')	3–8	1–1½ ft.
DAYLILY (*Hemerocallis* cvs.)	3–10	1½–3 ft.
LATE-BLOOMING ASTILBE (*Astilbe chinensis* 'Sister Theresa' and *A. chinensis* 'Visions')	4–8	1½–2 ft.
'MAY NIGHT' GARDEN SAGE (*Salvia × sylvestris* 'May Night')	5–9	2–ft.
PINKS (*Dianthus* spp. and cvs.)	3–10	½–2 ft.
SEDUM (*Sedum* 'Autumn Joy')	3–10	1½–2 ft.
SEDUM (*Sedum spectabile* 'Brilliant')	4–9	1½–2 ft.
ST. JOHN'S WORT (*Hypericum* spp. and cvs.)	5–9	1–4 ft.
YARROW (*Achillea* spp. and cvs.)	3–9	2–3 ft.
MEDIUM		
BEE BALM (*Monarda* spp. and cvs.)	4–9	3–4 ft.
'BONICA' ROSE (*Rosa* 'Bonica')	4–9	3–4 ft.
FOXGLOVE (*Digitalis purpurea* and cvs.)	4–8	3–6 ft.
KNOCK OUT ROSE (*Rosa* Radrazz)	5–9	3–4 ft.
'MARTHA'S VINEYARD' ROSE (*Rosa* 'Martha's Vineyard')	4–9	3–4 ft.
MICHAELMAS DAISY (*Aster novi-belgii* cvs.)	4–8	3–4 ft.
ORIENTAL LILY (*Lilium* 'Star Gazer', *L.* 'Mediterranee', and *L.* 'Golden Elegance')	4–8	3–5 ft.
PURPLE CONEFLOWER (*Echinacea purpurea* 'Magnus')	3–9	4–5 ft.
RUSSIAN SAGE (*Perovskia atriplicifolia*)	6–9	4–5 ft.
SUMMER PHLOX (*Phlox paniculata* 'Eva Cullum' and 'David')	4–8	3–4 ft.
LARGE		
BUTTERFLY BUSH (*Buddleia davidii* cvs.)	6–9	8–10 ft.
HOLLYHOCK (*Alcea rosea* cvs.)	3–9	5–8 ft.
HYDRANGEA (*Hydrangea* spp. and cvs.)	4–9	3–10 ft.
ROSE OF SHARON (*Hibiscus syriacus* and cvs.)	5–9	8–10 ft.

'Nikko Blue' hydrangea

Hollyhock

'Star Gazer' Oriental lily

'Magnus' purple coneflower

'Becky' Shasta daisy

'Moonshine' yarrow

CONTRAST PROVIDES VISUAL IMPACT

One benefit of moving plants around so much in the early years of my garden was that it gave me a chance to experiment with different combinations. After much trial and error, I discovered that plants with contrasting shapes, textures, and colors made good partners. For example, when I moved some black-eyed Susans next to a large clipped boxwood, their bright blooms seemed to leap out of the garden. I realized that the sharp contrast between the bold flowers and the boxwood's deep green foliage and formal, mounded shape made them good partners. Inspired by this discovery, I began to pair other contrasting plants. I found that peonies—with their dark green, glossy leaves and tidy, rounded habit—make a wonderful foil for the feathery foliage of yarrow and the sprawling habit of catmint. Peonies also work well next to the swordlike foliage of bearded irises and the tall, slender flower stalks of foxgloves and lilies. Similarly, I planted *Sedum spectabile* 'Brilliant', which resembles a light green ball for most of the summer, next to the spiky blooms of 'May Night' sage. Behind the sedum I planted a clump of vase-shaped Shasta daisies. In addition to the contrasting shapes of these three perennials, I like the graceful succession of flowering times they offer beginning in early spring when the 'May Night' sage begins to bloom. In July, the daisies get to strut their stuff. When the daisies begin to fade in August, the broccoli-like flower heads of 'Brilliant' take center stage, changing from green to lavender-pink and drawing attention away from the deadheaded daisies.

Relying on long-blooming workhorses lets me trade my garden gloves for a cool drink while I sit back and enjoy the beautiful view. That's my kind of garden.

SPECTACULAR POOLSIDE PLANTING TIPS

My friends always want to pick my brain about landscape design; Jonnelle is no exception, especially now that she owns a new home with a swimming pool. She invited me over to see her typical bare-bones backyard: medium size with a spacious concrete deck, a patio table, a couple of chaise longues, and one old lemon tree. Behind the pool, a cedar fence and a strip of grass provided no privacy from the two-story house next door. "Is there enough room to plant anything in such a small space?" she asked. "And can we create privacy and screen the neighbor's house?"

My designer's mind knew that to transform her flat boring space, the area would need some serious volume and diversity. Without any plantings, the yard lacked a backdrop with nothing to frame the view of the pool or soften the transition of the surrounding concrete patio. Even with these complications at hand, I was able to suggest some creative and flexible solutions sure to satisfy Jonnelle and any plantcentric gardener with a similar situation.

When selecting a plant palette, it is important to choose those that keep the pool and deck clean and safe. So stay away from potential problem plants that:

- Drop messy debris that could clog the filter
- Have berries or fruit that could stain the patio
- Have invasive roots that could compromise the pool structure
- Attract bees, to reduce the chances of being stung while soaking in the sun
- Have thorns that romping kids could fall into
- Are susceptible to disease (sprays applied to the plants could end up in the pool)
- Can't tolerate exposure to pool chemicals

With that said, you have plenty from which to choose.

CREATE A SENSE OF VOLUME
Equally space three patio trees in the center of the narrow bed behind the pool. As they mature, the canopies will fill in and create a privacy screen from tall structures, like the neighbor's house. Choose trees with polite root systems, a trunk girth of no more than 6 in. to 8 in. diameter, and a maximum height of 15 ft. to 20 ft. at maturity.

CREATE A COHESIVE LOOK
Intersperse a few of the same plants on both sides of the trees to add uniformity. Choose evergreen shrubs with unique or contrasting foliage for appeal all year. Keep pruning maintenance to a minimum by selecting shrubs with a naturally pleasing form and manageable size.

FRAME THE BED WITH COLOR
In contrast to the rigid backdrop, a lower layer of flowering annuals or perennials adds dimension and interest to the design. Fill in any bare spots with ground covers to keep exposed soil from blowing into the water

DRESS UP THE DECK WITH POTS
Incorporating container plants around the swimming pool boosts the sculptural element and incorporates opportunities for seasonal color. Arrange odd numbers of pots in clusters, or use three identical containers in a row as a striking focal point. Have fun with the character of your containers, but stay true to the style of your home.

JAZZ UP A BORDER
WITH SHRUBS

For a surefire way to add pizzazz to your border, add shrubs. These showy plants strut their stuff from season to season. Horticulturist and author Erica Glasener profiles seven of the best shrub choices.

BECAUSE MY GARDEN IS SMALL, I TREAT IT LIKE A LARGE MIXED border where trees, shrubs, perennials, annuals, and bulbs all peacefully coexist. Not having a lot of room for plants also means that I have to be discriminating. When it comes to choosing shrubs, I opt for those that offer more than just one season of interest. I look for ones with distinctive foliage, flowers, fragrance, or bark that can add interest to the garden year-round. I want them to be easy to tend as well. Here are seven that I think make the cut. Pick shrubs like smokebush for the visual drama it creates, or hydrangea or buttercup winterhazel for their early bloom time. Elderberry is striking in summer, and weigela shines from spring through fall.

Shrubs like 'Velvet Cloak' smokebush make a striking accent to the garden.

SMOKEBUSH OFFERS SPRING BLOOMS AND FALL COLOR

When *Cotinus coggygria* (USDA Hardiness Zones 5–8) blooms, it looks like clouds of pink smoke, hence its common name. Although the actual flowers are tiny, the panicles put on a show beginning as early as June and lasting into August or September. Growing 10 feet to 15 feet tall and nearly as wide, smokebush has an open habit and rounded, medium green leaves, 1½ inches to 3½ inches long. I particularly like the purple-leaved forms. 'Royal Purple' has leaves that start out maroon and get darker as the season progresses, culminating with a spectacular display of red-purple in the fall. The leaves of 'Velvet Cloak' are dark purple throughout the growing season, turning more of a red-purple in autumn.

Both cultivars make a striking accent or focal point in the mixed border with other shrubs and perennials like Russian sage (*Perovskia atriplicifolia*, Zones 6–9) or sage (*Salvia guaranitica*, Zones 8–10). Plant this undemanding shrub in well-drained soil in full sun to partial shade.

Controlling a smokebush's size is as simple as pruning it to the ground in spring. This promotes vigorous, deeply colored foliage but sacrifices flower buds (which sprout from two-year-old wood). To have the best of both worlds, cut back only one-third of the shrub every year, which will provide beautiful foliage while saving some flower buds.

'TARDIVA' HYDRANGEA BLOOMS IN LATE SUMMER

One of my all-time favorite hydrangeas is also one of the easiest to grow. 'Tardiva' hydrangea (*Hydrangea paniculata* 'Tardiva', Zones 4–8) has large, white, cone-shaped blooms; I have measured panicles that were 12 inches long. The blooms start out white, fade to pink, then turn to brown. Most important, it flowers at a time when few other shrubs are blooming—as early as August and as late as September, depending on where you live. The blooms fade with the onset of winter and dry on the shrub, providing interest in the winter landscape.

This hydrangea blooms on the current year's growth, which means that the best time to prune is in early spring just as new growth is beginning. You can cut stems back to 12 inches long or less, and in no time you will have a mature shrub 6 feet tall or higher. As the flowers appear on my shrub at the ends of the branches, the entire plant arches gracefully like a big bouquet in the middle of my garden.

'Tardiva' hydrangea, unlike other hydrangeas, can take full sun even in the South, so feel free to give it any exposure other than deep shade. For a white garden, plant it in combination with 'Honorine Jobert' anemone (*Anemone × hybrida* 'Honorine Jobert,' Zones 4–8) and 'Prince' aster (<*Aster lateriflorus* 'Prince', Zones 4–8), the latter of which has dark purple foliage and sprays of tiny white flowers with red-pink centers. For contrast, plant 'Tardiva' in combination with deep purple flowering asters.

CHOOSE BUTTERCUP WINTERHAZEL FOR ITS EARLY FLOWERS

Buttercup winterhazel (*Corylopsis pauciflora*, Zones 6–9) is a diminutive shrub, growing 4 feet to 6 feet tall and wide, with foliage that resembles a witch-hazel's and soft, fragrant yellow flowers that bloom in early spring. Its slender branches create an interesting winter sculpture. This reliable shrub grows in full sun or light shade. The only pruning you need to do is to remove the occasional errant branch. After four years, my plant has made a small arching shrub.

Plant it in front of evergreens in the middle or front of the border or next to a dwarf Hinoki cypress (*Chamaecyparis obtusa* 'Nana', Zones 4–8). Early bulbs like *Iris reticulata* cvs. (Zones 5–8) and small daffodils also make good companions for buttercup winterhazel. Another garden-worthy species with fragrant yellow flowers is *Corylopsis glabrescens* (Zones 6–9). It grows 8 feet to 15 feet tall and almost as wide, so it may not be suitable for small borders.

JAPANESE SUMMERSWEET IS A WINNER IN EVERY SEASON

While summersweet (*Clethra alnifolia*, Zones 3–9) is a popular shrub for summer blooms, its cousin Japanese summersweet (*Clethra barbinervis*, Zones 6–8) offers not only fragrant flowers but also shiny gray and brown bark. As it matures, the bark peels, exposing its various shades. A standout in the winter landscape, this large shrub grows 10 feet to 15 feet high. In late summer, usually from July to August, it produces 4-inch- to 6-inch-long panicles of fragrant white flowers at the tips of its branches. In autumn, the leaves turn from green to yellow, making this shrub a winner in every season.

'Tardiva' hydrangea

Japanese summersweet

DESIGNING WITH SHRUBS

Shrubs can serve myriad roles in a garden—on their own or in combination with other shrubs. Here are a few examples.

ANCHORS

Create part of a border's structural backbone by using shrubs as anchors. Well-placed shrubs tie a design together, supporting other plants throughout the seasons with a consistent presence and a sense of scale. 'Henry's Garnet' Virginia sweetspire planted with evergreens like the native inkberry (*Ilex glabra* 'Compacta', Zones 5–9) can give a planting a cohesive feeling.

FOCAL POINTS

Some shrubs are so eye catching that, depending on the season, they become a focal point in a border. In early spring, the delicate flowers of buttercup winterhazel are a highlight. Later in the season, smokebush takes the spotlight with its cloud of pink blooms. By late summer, the huge white flowers of 'Tardiva' hydrangea demand to be noticed. In a woodland garden, Japanese summersweet can serve as a strong vertical focal point.

DEFINERS OF SPACE

Shrubs can also define garden spaces. To punctuate a border with a beginning and an end, use the same shrub, like a 'Black Beauty' elderberry with its dark foliage, at both ends.

BACKDROPS

Old-fashioned weigela planted at the back of the border, in combination with evergreens, provides an effective foil for herbaceous plants placed in front.

Like all members of the genus *Clethra*, Japanese summersweet prefers partial shade and moist, fertile soil but tolerates a wide range of growing conditions including full sun. If you find this shrub's height intimidating or the shrub itself is getting a little too big for you, simply cut out the oldest and tallest stems or any that stray too wide.

Plant it in a woodland garden with ferns, native azaleas, and Lenten roses (*Helleborus* × *hybridus* cvs., Zones 6–9), or place it at the back of a sunny border in combination with perennials that bloom in late summer, such as Joe Pye weed (*Eupatorium purpureum*, Zones 3–9).

ELDERBERRIES ARE STRIKING IN SUMMER

For a shrub with bold and colorful foliage, flowers, and berries, you can choose among any of the forms of either the European elder (*Sambucus nigra* and cvs., Zones 6–8) or the American elderberry (*S. canadensis* and cvs., Zones 4–9). These multistemmed shrubs make striking focal points. Their deeply divided leaves—each has seven 2-inch- to 6-inch-long leaflets—add interesting texture to the border, especially the colorful forms like *S. nigra* 'Black Beauty'. In early summer, masses of lemon-scented pink flowers stand out against purple-black foliage.

For the best results, plant elderberries in full sun and moist soil. The mature size varies greatly, from 5 feet to 20 feet tall and wide, according to the specific cultivar and its location. 'Black Beauty' and others can be treated like hardy perennials and cut back hard in the fall where I live, but check with a local nursery or extension office first to see if this shrub can be handled this way in your area.

'HENRY'S GARNET' SWEETSPIRE HAS COLOR IN SPRING AND FALL

You can't go wrong with 'Henry's Garnet' Virginia sweetspire (*Itea virginica* 'Henry's Garnet', Zones 6–9). This adaptable native grows in full sun or partial shade and tolerates wet or dry soil. Growing 3 feet to 6 feet high and 1½ times as wide, it propagates itself by suckering. Clusters of slightly fragrant white flowers, up to 6 inches long, cover the plant in late spring. True to its name, its foliage turns garnet in autumn.

American elderberry

Weigela florida 'Variegata'

Site it at the edge of a pond or on a bank to help control erosion. If it spreads beyond where you would like it to grow, the suckers can be easily dug up and given to friends that have yet to discover this charmer.

CHOOSE WEIGELA FOR THREE SEASONS OF LEAVES

Old-fashioned weigela (*Weigela florida* and cvs., Zones 5–8) comes in a large variety of flavors. The numerous cultivars include types with variegated foliage (*W. florida* 'Variegata') and dark-leaved forms (*W. florida* 'Wine and Roses'). The only time this shrub doesn't shine is in the winter when it loses its foliage. It is best used as part of a mixed planting that also includes evergreen shrubs. For a bright accent, try the cultivar 'Rubidor' with its chartreuse foliage and ruby red flowers. I have especially admired it in combination with blue atlas cedar (*Cedrus atlantica* f. *glauca*, Zones 6–9).

Plant weigela in full sun in well-drained soil. It ranges in size from 3 feet to 9 feet tall and up to 12 feet across, depending on the selection. A spring bloomer with funnel-shaped flowers, it blooms on last year's branches.

BEST BORDER SHRUBS

PLANT NAME	BLOOM TIME	ZONES
BUTTERCUP WINTERHAZEL (*Corylopsis pauciflora*)	Early to midspring	6–9
ELDERBERRY (*Sambucus nigra* cvs. and *S. canadensis* cvs.)	Early to midsummer	4–9
'HENRY'S GARNET' SWEETSPIRE (*Itea virginica* 'Henry's Garnet')	Late spring to summer	6–9
JAPANESE SUMMERSWEET (*Clethra barbinervis*)	Middle to late summer	6–8
SMOKEBUSH (*Cotinus coggygria* and cvs.)	Summer	5–8
'TARDIVA' HYDRANGEA (*Hydrangea paniculata* 'Tardiva')	Late summer to fall	4–8
WEIGELA (*Weigela florida* cvs.)	Late spring to early summer	5–8

✓ ADD SHRUBS AND TREES
✓ DESIGN IDEAS
✓ PLANTS FOR SUN

A FOCUS ON
TREES AND SHRUBS

Inspired by his client's collection of trees, garden designer Mike Donnally designed a border in which Japanese maples were the stars of the show. He shares how he focused more attention on them by adding a dazzling cast of supporting shrubs and plants.

WHEN I BEGAN WORKING WITH ONE OF MY LANDSCAPE CLIENTS, he had been building his collection of trees and shrubs for many years. They had been assembled with little rhyme or reason, so he asked me to give the collection a sense of composition.

Of all the trees my client had amassed, he valued his Japanese maples the most, so these became the basis for my design. To show off the maples' exquisite palette of color, form, and texture, I created a large crescent-shaped border behind his house to serve as a "gallery." But rather than just lining them up in rows to be viewed as individual plants, I wanted the maples to be part of a pleasing ensemble with some of the other plants in the collection (see the photo on p. 180). The overall size of the crescent border and the interior lawn it surrounds is about a ½ acre, with the inside line of the border measuring 300 feet (see the site plan on p. 180).

This space serves as an outdoor gallery to showcase exceptional trees and shrubs. A break in the border beckons you to enter.

Massive trees and shrubs make a magnificent statement. After 14 years, some plants in this border now stand as tall as 20 feet, providing a sense of enclosure. (B on site plan.)

FINDING THE PROPER PLACEMENT

Of the existing plantings, I planned to retain only three crabapples: a pair of weeping crabs (*Malus* 'Echtermeyer') that would flank the entry into the garden and an upright crab (*M. floribunda*) that would serve as a spring focal point in one of the beds.

My client and I first chose and placed 12 maples from his collection to anchor this border. When I began, the maples ranged from 8 inches to 6 feet tall. I took care to place them so they would have room to grow to maturity and not be overshadowed by a neighbor. In addition, I positioned each one so that its overall character and outstanding attributes, such as the color and texture of the foliage, would be seen in the best light. Because the border was entirely in full sun, this gave me many options for placement. I knew that soft easterly morning light would enhance the delicacy of a filigree-textured maple (*Acer palmatum* 'Atrolineare'), so I put it in the eastern part of the crescent. On the other hand, it takes stronger afternoon light to reveal the veining and color of the dark burgundy–leaved maples (such as *Acer palmatum* 'Trompenburg'), so I planted those in the border's western section.

CREATING A CONTRASTING BACKGROUND

After I situated the Japanese maples in the border, I started thinking about supporting plants. To emphasize the seasonal changes of the deciduous maples, I looked to evergreens (see the top photo on the facing page) to provide a steady presence year round and to act as a backdrop for the maples' foliage as well as for their bare branches in winter. I envisioned large, broad evergreens as backdrops and narrow, vertical evergreens to contrast with the maples' rounded canopies.

As I considered evergreens, I drew on my experience growing many trees and shrubs, consulted woody-plant references, and talked with other gardeners. I thought

A crescent-shaped border turns a collection of trees into an ensemble.

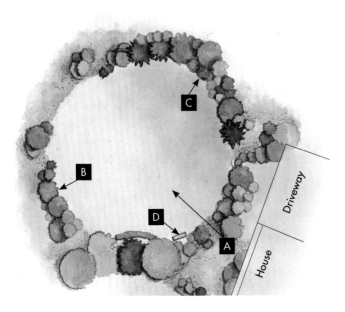

about how the habits of potential partners would mature in 5 years, 10 years, even 20 years. I also paid attention to attributes such as the color and texture of foliage and bark.

The first supporting plants I selected were a number of gold threadleaf false cypresses (*Chamaecyparis pisifera* 'Filifera Aurea'). I placed them in groups and as individual plants throughout the bed. Initially they were only 1 foot tall and wide and were planted on 8-foot centers. Now, 14 years later, they are 10 feet to 12 feet tall and up to 8 feet wide.

The repetition of their gold color, fine texture, and pyramidal form provides continuity and rhythm throughout the crescent garden. Watching them grow over the years, I've liked the way these gold false cypresses interact with the maples. The intense color of their summer growth against the burgundy maple foliage reminds me of the richness of gold jewelry worn on red silk. By providing contrast, their evergreen foliage also supports the exposed dormant forms of the Japanese maples in winter. When the sun breaks on dismal February days, the false cypresses really stand out.

FILLING IN THE GAPS

The Japanese maples and false cypresses set the tone and provided the backbone of this border, but it needed other elements to bring it to life. I introduced another supporting plant, gold arborvitae (*Thuja occidentalis* 'Watnong Gold'), at the midpoint of the crescent garden to add another dimension and to bridge the gap between the two weeping crabapples. The arborvitae's gold color repeated that of the golden false cypresses but with a variation in intensity. I was a little apprehensive about placing the gold arborvitaes between the crabapples because the crabs' blooms are a shade of pink, but there was enough purple in the flowers to serve as a sound color complement to the gold.

To deepen the composition further, I added other plantings over a three-year period. A silvery dwarf cedar (*Cedrus deodara* 'Snow Sprite') and three dark-leaved yak rhododendrons (*Rhododendron yakushimanum* 'Ken Janeck') brought new forms and colors to the bed. To complete this picture, a single golden full-moon maple (*Acer shirasawanum* 'Aureum') became an exclamation point, with its golden-chartreuse foliage.

To add some extra zest in spring and summer, I planted a few bulbs, annuals, and perennials in parts of the

Evergreens provide balance for deciduous plants. A 'Kasagiyama' Japanese maple, with its delicate burgundy leaves, is complemented by the upright foliage of a *Pinus cembra* 'Pygmaea' on the left and a fine-textured *Chamaecyparis pisifera* 'Filifera' on the right. (C on site plan.)

A bench provides a viewing place. Just as in an indoor gallery, a comfortable seat invites visitors to contemplate the display. (D on site plan.)

border that had yet to fill in. A cluster of white cleome (*Cleome hassleriana* 'Helen Campbell') beside the weeping crabapple is pretty for now, but to create long-lived flowery detail in this area of the border, I'm training a single pink gallica rose (*Rosa gallica* 'Complicata') to weave through a weeping crabapple. The mid-June blooms of 'Complicata' are reminiscent of the earlier purple-pink crabapple blossoms. The rose's blooms also fill in the gap in early summer before the crab's fruit begins deepening to purple in midsummer. This play of cyclic change is one of the things I relish about creating a woody border.

Planning and planting a large woody border has been a great way for this client to put his collection to work and to celebrate the year-round beauty of his remarkable trees and shrubs.

Moisture-loving plants thrive
in a bog garden. Be sure to
site it in full sun.

TUCK A BOG
INTO A BORDER

Want to add a little excitement to your border? Create a showcase for unusual plants—think carnivorous—by including a small bog in your garden. Jeff Jabco, coordinator of horticulture at Scott Arboretum, shares the secrets of his bog success with you.

TRAVELING TO GARDENS AND WILD PLACES OFTEN INSPIRES ME to try new, very different, things in my own garden. For example, I never imagined I'd grow bog plants—those that need to have their roots in standing water—until I saw them in nature. I was on a canoeing trip to the Boundary Waters of northern Minnesota when I saw my first wild rice, sundews, and pitcher plants. Later that year, I visited the New Jersey Pine Barrens and was surprised to find more of these bizarre plants. I also visited the North Carolina Botanical Garden in Chapel Hill, where a series of raised bogs made it easy for me to inspect the plants.

When my partner came home and said he was going to install a bog for the public garden where he worked, it seemed like fate was telling me we were destined to have a bog garden, too. We already had a pond nestled in the border at the back of our garden, so we decided to treat the bog the same way. Placing it right in one of our borders allows us to showcase pitcher plants and venus fly traps among our tree peonies and yews without having to give up much room.

Sarracenia leucophylla

that are constantly wet but aren't in flowing water. Many are located on hummocks that stick up out of the standing water on the marshy edges where water floods infrequently. We had sited our bog so that runoff would flow into the bed. Because bog plants don't have extensive root systems to anchor them, the plants were quickly dislodged when it rained heavily. Although the roots of these plants can handle constant moisture, the tops and crowns cannot. We eventually moved our bog to a sunnier site when it became clear that our original location wasn't working.

PICK SHOWY PLANTS

Once we found the right spot, we planted various plants in the bog and watered them in. Pitcher plants are the showiest plants in our bog because of their brightly colored pitchers and their large, long-lasting flower stalks. The pitchers can be deep red, bright green, yellow, or red and white variegated. Most of our bog plants are pitcher plants, including *Sarracenia rubra*, *S. purpurea*, and *S. flava* and hybrids between these and *S. leucophylla*, *S. minor*, *S. psittacina*, and *S. oreophila*. There are pitcher plants native from USDA Hardiness Zones 2 to 11, so there is one suited for every garden; they might, however, be a challenge to find commercially.

We also grow sundews (*Drosera* spp., Zones 3–9) and the native autumn-flowering orchid nodding ladies' tresses (*Spiranthes cernua* f. *odorata*, Zones 5–8). We plan to try bladderworts (*Utricularia* spp., Zones 3–10) and butterworts (*Pinguicula* spp., Zones 3–10) in the future.

SITE YOUR BOG IN FULL SUN

We learned some important lessons after installing our bog garden. The first one was that pitcher plants and most other carnivorous plants need at least 6 hours of direct sun a day. We put our bog behind a low, curved dry stone wall with a sitting area where we could observe these unusual plants up close. After several seasons, however, the bog became shaded, and the pitcher plants got smaller and flowered less.

The next lesson was that bog plants like moisture but shouldn't be situated in a low area where the water may wash through too vigorously. In nature these plants thrive on the edges of streams or ponds in areas

BOG MAINTENANCE

We are careful never to let the bog dry out. We water with collected rainwater because tap water may be too high in pH or contain minerals that are detrimental to our bog plants. Pitcher plants, which are easy to care for, are carnivorous, getting their nutrients from water and soil and by digesting captured insects. We sometimes help nature by disposing of smaller insects like mosquitoes or flies into the pitchers. We also fertilize the bog garden with quarter-strength water-soluble fertilizer, which we apply with a watering can monthly during the growing season, stopping in August.

Once the soil is sufficiently cold (usually after January 1), I cut the branches off our Christmas tree and place them

Bog garden plants like the sundew at left and the pitcher plant above need a wet area with fairly still water and at least 6 hours of direct sun a day.

HOW TO MAKE A BOG

Bogs are constructed like a pond but are much easier to maintain, because with a bog you don't have to be concerned about water circulation, the growth of algae, or a slow leak in the liner. To install our bog, we dug a 24-inch-deep hole with relatively steep sides in the shape we wanted. We then lined the hole with the flexible black plastic used to line ponds. We set the liner in place with enough material to reach the edge of the hole.

Because the bog should maintain a consistent water level, there must be a way for excess water to drain. Some books recommend piercing the lower half of the liner with a few holes to let excess water slowly drain through or to use leftover scraps of pond liner to line the hole, overlapping them until the hole is completely lined with several layers so water can gradually seep out through the layers. In our bog, we placed the liner so that one section of the edge is just slightly lower than the rest of the rim, thus allowing excess water to slowly flow off the surface. This method has worked well for us.

After the lining was installed, we filled the bog with a special soil mix. Bog plants require a low-fertility, acidic soil that replicates the sphagnum moss bogs where they grow. We attempted to get this acidic condition by using a 3-to-1 mixture of peat moss to coarse sand (or we could have used coarse perlite instead of sand). We thoroughly moistened the peat moss before mixing it with the sand, then we filled the bog to the top of the liner with the mixture, making a slight mound in the center. We let the soil settle for several weeks, keeping it constantly moist, before we planted anything.

around and lightly over the plants to protect them from repeated freezing and thawing, which may heave them out of the soil. In early April, I remove the branches gradually over a period of a couple of weeks, then cut the old pitchers back to the crown. New flower buds arise shortly thereafter and quickly grow to flower from late May though mid-June. After the petals drop from the flowers, the large seed pods remain, so the flowers still appear to be in bloom. New pitchers begin to grow in May. The nodding ladies' tresses also get cut back to the crown in spring, but the sundews are tiny and don't need cutting back.

We grow hundreds of plants in our garden, but the bog is one of our favorite spots and the one that attracts the most attention from visitors.

PLANTING GALLERY

PLAY WITH
COLOR AND FORM

THE GOAL OF THIS BED—LOCATED IN FULL SUN—WAS TO BE A focal point, with strong color and form but also a naturalized effect. To create it, an interesting mix of three allium cultivars with varying bloom times was used. The variety of bloom times extends the impact of the planting. A vibrant, contrasting background highlights the bold shapes of the allium blooms in the foreground. Layers of different textures and colors draw visitors close to get a good look.

Garden designer: Jonathan Wright, Wayne, Pennsylvania

THE PLANTS

1 'Gladiator' allium (*Allium* 'Gladiator', Zones 4–8)

2 'Purple Sensation' allium (*Allium* 'Purple Sensation', Zones 4–9)

3 'Globemaster' allium (*Allium* 'Globemaster', Zones 6–10)

4 'Ogon' spirea (*Spiraea thunbergii* 'Ogon', USDA Hardiness Zones 5–8)

5 'Rose Glow' Japanese barberry (*Berberis thunbergii* 'Rose Glow', Zones 5–8)

6 'Countess Helen von Stein' lambs' ears (*Stachys byzantina* 'Countess Helen von Stein', Zones 4–8)

7 Sedge (*Carex flagellifera*, Zones 7–9)

8 'Golden Sword' yucca (*Yucca filamentosa* 'Golden Sword', Zones 4–11)

9 'Sapphire' blue oat grass (*Helictotrichon sempervirens* 'Sapphire', Zones 4–9)

PLANTS
AND A PATHWAY
CONTROL THE VIEW

CREATED IN A SUBURBAN BACKYARD, THIS GARDEN IS MEANT TO screen a children's play set and a neighbor's two-story house and to provide a pathway to an office. Two tall trees block the view and anchor the beds, which are filled in with shrubs and perennials the homeowner loves. To achieve some subtle symmetry, plants, textures, and forms were repeated from side to side, and a rose-covered arbor embraces the brick walkway, creating continuity. The curving pathway makes the garden seem larger than it is because the eye can catch only a glimpse of what's around the bend.

Garden designer: Rebecca Sweet, Los Altos, California

THE PLANTS

1 Jacaranda tree (*Jacaranda mimosifolia*, USDA Hardiness Zones 9–11)

2 Oriental fountain grass (*Pennisetum orientale*, Zones 6–10)

3 Daisy bush (*Senecio greyi*, syn. *Brachyglottis greyi*, Zones 9–10)

4 Japanese forest grass (*Hakonechloa macra*, Zones 5–9)

5 'Biokovo' hardy geranium (*Geranium × cantabrigiense* 'Biokovo', Zones 5–8)

6 Fourth of July™ large-flowered climbing rose (*Rosa* 'WEKroalt', Zones 5–9)

7 Sunny Delight® boxleaf euonymus (*Euonymus japonicus* var. *microphyllus* 'Moncliff', Zones 6–9)

8 'Debutante' camellia (*Camellia japonica* 'Debutante', Zones 7–10)

9 'Golf Ball' kohuhu (*Pittosporum tenuifolium* 'Golf Ball', Zones 9–11)

10 Mimosa tree (*Albizia julibrissin* var. *rosea*, Zones 6–9)

11 Red Abyssinian banana (*Ensete ventricosum* 'Maurelii', Zones 9–11)

12 'Amy' hebe (*Hebe* 'Amy', Zones 9–11)

13 Ogon' sweet flag (*Acorus gramineus* 'Ogon', Zones 6–9)

14 Blue echeveria (*Echeveria glauca*, Zones 8–11)

15 'Heavenly Blue' prostrate speedwell (*Veronica prostrata* 'Heavenly Blue', Zones 5–8)

16 Bloodroot (*Sanguinaria canadensis*, Zones 3–9)

BLUR THE LINE BETWEEN GARDEN AND WOODS

THIS SHADY, EDGE-OF-THE-WOODS BED SERVES AS A TRANSITION between cultivated space and wilderness. Two mature white pines were removed to open a window into the woods. Then the border was planted with a mix of woodland plants studded with a few bold punches of texture and color. Annuals, like coleus and impatiens, serve to fill in spaces left behind by spring ephemerals, such as Virginia bluebell (*Mertensia virginica*, USDA Hardiness Zones 3–7), trillium (*Trillium* spp. and cvs., Zones 4–9), and Grecian windflower (*Anemone blanda* cvs., Zones 4–8). The ornaments tie the planting back to civilization, while the fallen log echoes the trees beyond. The butterfly bench beckons visitors into this transition zone, where they can feel like a part of the woods without losing their connection to civilization.

Garden designer: Janet Macunovich, Bloomfield Hills, Michigan

THE PLANTS

1 'Rustic Orange' coleus (*Solenostemon scutellarioides* 'Rustic Orange', Zone 11)

2 Goatsbeard (*Aruncus aethusifolius*, Zones 3–9)

3 'Accent White' impatiens (*Impatiens walleriana* 'Accent White', annual)

4 Full-moon maple (*Acer japonicum* 'Aconitifolium', Zones 5–7)

5 'Roseum' epimedium (*Epimedium* × *youngianum* 'Roseum', Zones 5–9)

6 Vernal sweet pea (*Lathyrus vernus*, Zones 5–7)

7 'Sizzler Red' salvia (*Salvia splendens* 'Sizzler Red', annual)

8 Yellow corydalis (*Corydalis lutea*, Zones 5–8)

9 Variegated brunnera (*Brunnera macrophylla* 'Variegata', Zones 3–7)

10 Elephant's ear (*Colocasia esculenta*, Zones 8–11)

11 Japanese painted fern (*Athyrium nipponicum* var. *pictum*, Zones 5–8)

COLOR MAKES A PLANTING COME TOGETHER

PINK IS ONE OF THE TRICKIEST COLORS TO WORK WITH. WITH SO MANY pinks in the plant world, making true color matches is a challenge, Diane Schaub explains. Her solution is to echo several similar shades in contrasting flower and foliage forms. A smattering of pale yellow-greens downplays the slight differences between the pinks. In this full-sun bed, the dusty pink tones of the hyssop are echoed in the deep burgundy blades of the fountain grass, while the colors of the lantana flowers tie together the neighboring pinks and the yellow-greens of the flowering tobacco and the plectranthus.

Garden designer: Diane Schaub, Central Park's Conservancy Garden, New York City

THE PLANTS

1 'Pink Frost' sweet potato vine (*Ipomoea batatas* 'Pink Frost', Zone 11)

2 'Lime Green' flowering tobacco (*Nicotiana alata* 'Lime Green', annual)

3 'Tutti Frutti' hyssop (*Agastache* 'Tutti Frutti', USDA Hardiness Zones 6–10)

4 'Pink Caprice' lantana (*Lantana camara* 'Pink Caprice', Zone 11)

5 Purple fountain grass (*Pennisetum setaceum* 'Rubrum', Zones 8–11)

6 'Green on Green' plectranthus (*Plectranthus forsteri* 'Green on Green', Zone 11)

FABULOUS FOLIAGE
LIGHTS UP THE SHADE

WHEN DESIGNING THIS 6-FOOT-LONG AND 3-FOOT-DEEP BED TO FLANK A shady patio, Holly Shaffer's goal was to provide an appealing entrance to this restful space and to give the patio a sense of enclosure without blocking the view of the rest of the garden. The waist-high planting is a textural mix of perennials and tender plants designed to entice. The fuzzy leaves of silver plectranthus beckon visitors to touch, while the northern sea oats rustle in the breeze, the flowing Japanese forest grass brings to mind soothing waters, and the Rex begonia excites the eyes. The mix of colors is compelling but soothing with minimal input from flowers, which helps the bed shine all season long.

Garden designer: Holly Shaffer, Kent, Ohio

THE PLANTS

1. Japanese forest grass (*Hakonechloa macra* 'Aureola', Zones 5–9)

2. Northern sea oats (*Chasmanthium latifolium*, USDA Hardiness Zones 5–9)

3. Silver plectranthus (*Plectranthus argentatus*, Zones 10–11)

4. 'Fairy' Rex begonia (*Begonia* 'Fairy', Zone 11)

5. 'Lemon Lime' hosta (*Hosta* 'Lemon Lime', Zones 3–9)

6. Lady fern (*Athyrium filix-femina*, Zones 4–9)

7. 'Milky Way' lungwort (*Pulmonaria* 'Milky Way', Zones 4–9)

AN EXCITING BED
FOR A HIGH-PROFILE AREA

GARDENER OR NOT, WHO DOESN'T LOVE A COTTAGE GARDEN? After all, its simplicity and charm are hard to resist. This casual and cheerful bed on a pedestrian-heavy street is perfectly matched to its cottagey seaside location, and its few plants are easily recognizable and a cinch to grow. The pleasing array of pastel pinks and purples is given a fresh accent with patches of chartreuse from the lady's mantle. Located in full sun in soil that has been amended with generous servings of compost, this portion of the bed is approximately 10 feet long and 5 feet deep.

Garden designer: Janie McCabe, Madison, Connecticut

THE PLANTS

1 'Mystic Meidiland' shrub rose (*Rosa* 'Mystic Meidiland'®, USDA Hardiness Zones 4–11)

2 Lady's mantle (*Alchemilla mollis*, Zones 4–7)

3 Stars of Persia (*Allium cristophii*, Zones 5–8)

4 'Hidcote' English lavender (*Lavandula angustifolia* 'Hidcote', Zones 5–8)

5 'Rozanne' hardy geranium (*Geranium* 'Rozanne', Zones 4–7)

6 'Grosso' lavender (*Lavandula* × *intermedia* 'Grosso', Zones 5–8)

DEER-RESISTANT BED
THAT SHINES IN FALL AND WINTER

DEDICATED GARDENERS MAY FIND THEMSELVES EXTENSIVELY researching plants for their garden. That's what Nancy and John Matthews did. They needed plants that would succeed in a moist, full-sun, deer-ridden site and still provide color and interest all year round. This is especially important during the gray winters characteristic of the Midwest, where they live. With the help of Citizens for Conservation, an organization dedicated to land stewardship and conservation, Nancy and John chose a diverse mix of tough, beautiful plants that go the distance through the seasons. Plants like stephanandra, black-eyed Susan, Joe Pye weed, Shasta daisy, and feather reed grass offer subtle colors, textures, and movement with natural good looks that temper the formality of the house beyond. Austrian pines and Bradford pear add consistent color and structure, lending a sense of permanence that echoes the timelessness of their brick background.

Garden designers: Nancy and John Matthews, North Barrington, Illinois

THE PLANTS

1. Bradford pear (*Pyrus calleryana* 'Bradford', USDA Hardiness Zones 5–8)

2. 'Gateway' Joe Pye weed (*Eupatorium maculatum* 'Gateway', Zones 5–11)

3. 'Crispa' cutleaf stephanandra (*Stephanandra incisa* 'Crispa', Zones 3–8)

4. 'Becky' Shasta daisy (*Leucanthemum × superbum* 'Becky', Zones 5–8)

5. 'Karl Foerster' feather reed grass (*Calamagrostis × acutiflora* 'Karl Foerster', Zones 5–9)

6. Austrian pine (*Pinus nigra*, Zones 5–8)

7. 'Goldsturm' black-eyed Susan (*Rudbeckia fulgida* var. *sullivantii* 'Goldsturm', Zones 4–9)

AN ASIAN GARDEN
THAT FLAUNTS SOME FANCY SHRUBS

A TREASURED SHRUB IS ENHANCED BY A GARDEN DESIGNED to complement it. An Asian garden is the natural choice for highlighting treasured cloud-pruned conifers. Because many of the plants in this design either are evergreen or hold their shape into winter, this garden is interesting year-round. The majority of the plants in this garden are variations on green, so a punch of color from the flaming glorybower and dwarf pomegranate is a welcome dash of excitement. A sweeping tapestry of tidy, low-growing plants and river rocks in contrasting colors lets the living artwork shine without distraction.

Garden designer: Bill Pinkham, Coastal Virginia

THE PLANTS

1. Dwarf mondo grass (*Ophiopogon japonicus* 'Gyoku-ryu', USDA Hardiness Zones 7–10)

2. 'Shimpaku' Chinese juniper (*Juniperus chinensis* 'Shimpaku', Zones 3–9)

3. 'Peppermint Stick' variegated giant reed (*Arundo donax* 'Peppermint Stick', Zones 6–9)

4. Flaming glorybower (*Clerodendrum splendens*, Zone 11)

5. Big muhly grass (*Muhlenbergia lindheimeri*, Zones 7–10)

6. 'Georgia Blue' speedwell (*Veronica peduncularis* 'Georgia Blue', Zones 6–8)

7. White rain lily (*Zephyranthes candida*, Zones 7–10)

8. Dwarf pomegranate (*Punica granatum* var. *nana*, Zones 7–10)

9. 'Hetzii Glauca' Chinese juniper (*Juniperus chinensis* 'Hetzii Glauca', Zones 3–9)

10. Dragon-eye Japanese red pine (*Pinus densiflora* 'Oculus Draconis', Zones 4–7)

11. 'Blueberry Muffin' Indian hawthorn (*Rhaphiolepis umbellata* 'Blueberry Muffin', Zones 8–11)

12. 'Kingsville Dwarf' littleleaf boxwood (*Buxus microphylla* 'Kingsville Dwarf', Zones 6–9)

13. 'San Gabriel' dwarf heavenly bamboo (*Nandina domestica* 'San Gabriel', Zones 6–11)

14. Mouse-ear hawkweed (*Hieracium pilosella*, Zones 5–9)

A FANTASTIC
FALL PLANTING
THAT'S DROUGHT TOLERANT TOO

DRY SUMMERS TAKE A TOLL ON PLANTS, SO ANY BORDER THAT will shine at the end of the season and on into fall has to be filled with some tough customers. This bed fills the bill. It puts on a spectacular show in late summer and fall, when the garden is used the most, and provides evergreen, drought-tolerant color year-round. While gold and burgundy are the most prevalent, the coppery fall color of the Japanese stewartia serves as a focal point, an added bonus to the tree's summertime camellia-like blooms. All of the plants thrive in the bed's full morning sun and afternoon shade. The bed's flat-stone edging provides an easy surface to mow over and hides a French drain that prevents water from reaching the house's foundation.

Garden designer: Stacie Crooks, Seattle, Washington

THE PLANTS

1 Common boxwood (*Buxus sempervirens*, Zones 6–8)

2 'Tuscan Blue' rosemary (*Rosmarinus officinalis* 'Tuscan Blue', Zones 8–11)

3 Japanese stewartia (*Stewartia pseudocamellia*, Zones 5–8)

4 Italian blue cypress (*Cupressus sempervirens* 'Glauca', Zones 7–9)

5 'Royal Cloak' Japanese barberry (*Berberis thunbergii* 'Royal Cloak', Zones 5–8)

6 'Professor Anton Kippenberg' Michaelmas daisy (*Aster novi-belgii* 'Professor Anton Kippenberg', Zones 4–8)

7 'Archer's Gold' lemon thyme (*Thymus x citriodorus* 'Archer's Gold', Zones 6–9)

8 Woolly thyme (*Thymus pseudolanuginosus*, Zones 5–9)

9 Magic Carpet spirea (*Spiraea japonica* 'Walbuma', Zones 4–9)

10 'Goldsturm' black-eyed Susan (*Rudbeckia fulgida* var. *sullivantii* 'Goldsturm', Zones 4–9)

11 'Gracillimus' miscanthus (*Miscanthus sinensis* 'Gracillimus', Zones 4–9)

12 Siberian iris (*Iris* cv., Zones 3–9)

13 'Autumn Joy' sedum (*Sedum* 'Autumn Joy', USDA Hardiness Zones 3–11)

A PURPOSEFUL
POOLSIDE PLANTING

THE MARK OF A GOOD DESIGN IS THAT IT ACCOMPLISHES A number of goals. Here, a range of heights and textures softens and partially obscures an overpowering mass of rock. The plants were chosen to withstand a hot, baking site in full sun by a swimming pool. And to ensure that the bed always offers something to look at, long-blooming plants like persicarias and daylilies were used to keep this bed interesting for the long haul, while the evergreens and grasses carry the bed through the winter. Despite often-dry conditions, the bed gets its fair share of moisture from an irrigation system.

Garden Design: Tom Peace, Denver, Colorado

THE PLANTS

1 Upright juniper (*Juniperus* cv., USDA Hardiness Zones 2–9)

2 Columnar blue spruce (*Picea pungens* cv., Zones 2–8)

3 'Morning Light' miscanthus (*Miscanthus sinensis* 'Morning Light', Zones 4–9)

4 Blue oat grass (*Helictotrichon sempervirens*, Zones 4–9)

5 Tall verbena (*Verbena bonariensis*, Zones 7–11)

6 'Happy Thought' geranium (*Pelargonium* 'Happy Thought', Zones 11)

7 Joe Pye weed (*Eupatorium purpureum*, Zones 3–9)

8 'Globosa' dwarf blue spruce (*Picea pungens* 'Globosa', Zones 2–8)

9 Plumbago (*Ceratostigma plumbaginoides*, Zones 5–9)

10 Blue sage (*Salvia azurea* ssp. *pitcheri*, Zones 5–9)

11 'Zing Rose' maiden pink (*Dianthus deltoides* 'Zing Rose', Zones 3–10)

12 'Firetail' persicaria (*Persicaria amplexicaulis* 'Firetail', Zones 3–8)

13 'Butterfly Blue' scabious (*Scabiosa columbaria* 'Butterfly Blue', Zones 3–8)

USDA HARDINESS ZONE MAP

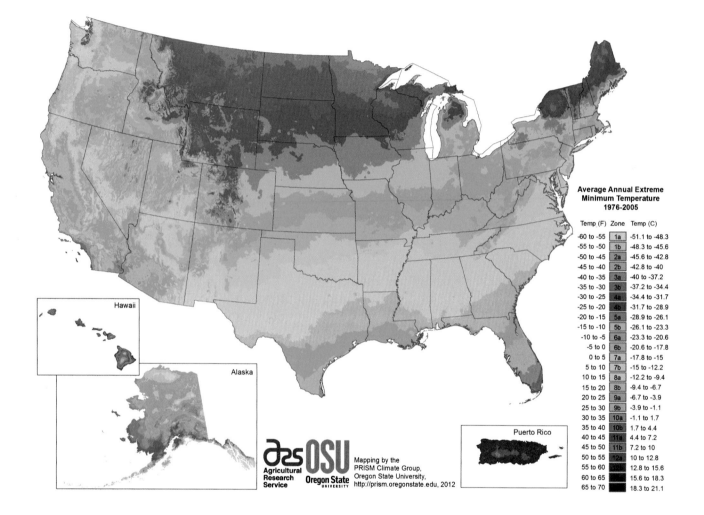

Average Annual Extreme Minimum Temperature 1976-2005

Temp (F)	Zone	Temp (C)
-60 to -55	1a	-51.1 to -48.3
-55 to -50	1b	-48.3 to -45.6
-50 to -45	2a	-45.6 to -42.8
-45 to -40	2b	-42.8 to -40
-40 to -35	3a	-40 to -37.2
-35 to -30	3b	-37.2 to -34.4
-30 to -25	4a	-34.4 to -31.7
-25 to -20	4b	-31.7 to -28.9
-20 to -15	5a	-28.9 to -26.1
-15 to -10	5b	-26.1 to -23.3
-10 to -5	6a	-23.3 to -20.6
-5 to 0	6b	-20.6 to -17.8
0 to 5	7a	-17.8 to -15
5 to 10	7b	-15 to -12.2
10 to 15	8a	-12.2 to -9.4
15 to 20	8b	-9.4 to -6.7
20 to 25	9a	-6.7 to -3.9
25 to 30	9b	-3.9 to -1.1
30 to 35	10a	-1.1 to 1.7
35 to 40	10b	1.7 to 4.4
40 to 45	11a	4.4 to 7.2
45 to 50	11b	7.2 to 10
50 to 55	12a	10 to 12.8
55 to 60		12.8 to 15.6
60 to 65		15.6 to 18.3
65 to 70		18.3 to 21.1

Hawaii

Alaska

Puerto Rico

Agricultural Research Service

OSU Oregon State UNIVERSITY

Mapping by the PRISM Climate Group, Oregon State University, http://prism.oregonstate.edu, 2012

Those gardening in Canada should refer to the Plant Hardiness Zone Map created by the Canadian Forest Service, which can be found online at http://planthardiness.gc.ca.

SOURCES

Arrowhead Alpines
517-223-3581
www.arrowheadalpines.com

Busse Gardens
800-544-3192
www.bussegardens.com

California Carnivores
707-824-0433
www.californiacarnivores.com

Earthly Pursuits
410-496-2523
www.earthlypursuits.net

Fieldstone Gardens
207-923-3836
www.fieldstonegardens.com

Greer Gardens
800-548-0111
www.greergardens.com

Joy Creek Nursery
503-543-7474
www.joycreek.com

Plant Delights Nursery
919-772-4794
www.plantdelights.com

Richters Herbs
905-640-6677
www.richters.com

Siskiyou Rare Plant Nursery
541-535-7103
www.siskiyourareplantnursery.com

Well-Sweep Herb Farm
908-852-5390
www.wellsweep.com

CONTRIBUTORS

Ruth Adams served as managing editor for *The New York Botanical Garden Illustrated Encyclopedia of Horticulture* by Thomas C. Everett. She gardens in Sharon, Connecticut.

Barbara Blossom Ashmun, a former contributing editor to *Fine Gardening*, is a garden designer in Portland, Oregon.

Pam Baggett is a writer, photographer, and tropical plant expert. She lectures on tropicals and other garden topics for garden groups and horticultural societies.

Ray Baker is an interior designer and architect who gardens in Bethlehem, Connecticut.

Jennifer Benner is a garden writer and lecturer and former associate editor at *Fine Gardening* magazine.

Daryl Beyers is a professional landscaper and was a former assistant editor at *Fine Gardening* magazine.

Steve Carroll is a plant ecologist at Truman State University in Kirksville, Missouri.

C. Colston Burrell is a garden designer and an award-winning author of several gardening books, including *Hellebores: A Comprehensive Guide.*

Stephanie Cohen is a contributing editor to *Fine Gardening* who lives in Collegeville, Pennsylvania, and has a passion for perennials.

Mike Donnally is a garden designer from Fairfield, Connecticut.

Sydney Eddison is a writer, gardener, and lecturer who lives in Newtown, Connecticut.

Scott Endres is co-owner of Tangletown Gardens in Minneapolis, Minnesota.

Amy Fahmy is a landscape architect who now works with the Biltmore Estate in Ashville, NC.

Stephen Gabor, along with Patrick Allen, is a principal of gabor + allen, a design-build practice in Venice, California.

Erica Glasener is a horticulturist, author, and hosted *A Gardener's Diary* on HGTV for 14 years.

Sue Hamilton is an associate professor of horticulture at the University of Tennessee in Knoxville and director of the University of Tennessee Gardens.

Andy Pulte is an arborist and horticulture instructor at the University of Tennessee.

Gordon Hayward is a garden designer based in Putney, Vermont.

Jeff Jabco is director of grounds and coordinator of horticulture for the Scott Arboretum of Swarthmore College, in Pennsylvania.

Suzanne Knutson is a landscape designer and garden writer in Fairfield County, Connecticut.

Rebecca Sams and her partner, Buell Steelman, own Mosaic Gardens, a landscape design-build firm in Eugene, Oregon.

Genevieve Schmidt is a landscape designer in Arcata, California.

Andrew Schulman is a landscape architect based in Seattle, Washington.

Bobbie Schwartz owns Bobbie's Green Thumb, a landscape design firm in Shaker Heights, Ohio.

Steve Silk, a garden designer and writer and managing editor, wings it in his garden in Farmington, Connecticut.

Cindy Stockett is a member of the Northwest Perennial Alliance and the Northwest Horticultural Society. She gardens in Vashon, Washington.

Linda Wesley is a former *Fine Gardening* associate editor from Newtown, Connecticut.

Jimmy Williams, garden columnist for *The Paris Post-Intelligencer*, gardens at his home in Paris, Tennessee.

CREDITS

All photos and illustrations are courtesy of *Fine Gardening* magazine © The Taunton Press, Inc., except as noted below:

vi: Photos by (top left) Virgina Small; (top right) Danielle Sherry; (bottom left) Michelle Gervais; (bottom right) Steve Aitken

pp. 4-11: Photos by © Allan Mandell

p. 9: Illustration by Melissa Lucas

pp. 12-17: Photos by Danielle Sherry

p. 18: Photos by Melissa Buntin

p. 20: Photos by Virgina Small

p. 21: Photos by (top) Steve Silk; (bottom) Melissa Rentin

p. 22: Photos by (top left and bottom) Virgina Small; (top right)Jennifer Benner

pp. 23-27: Photos by Virgina Small

p. 28: Photos by Jodie Delohery

p. 29: Photos by Virgina Small

pp. 30-35: Photos by ©Allan Mandell

p. 36-41: Photos by Brandi Spade

p. 42: Photos by Janet Jenmott

p. 44: Photos by (bottom) Melissa Lucas

p. 45: Photos by Melissa Lucas

p. 46: Photos by (top right and bottom left) Melissa Lucas; (bottom right) Jennifer Benner

p. 47: Photos by © Sydney Eddison

pp. 48-51: Photos by Virgina Small

p. 51: Illustration by Melissa Buntin

pp. 52-54: Photos by Steve Aitken

p. 55: Photos by Melissa Lucas

pp. 56-61: Photos by © Allan Mandell

p. 62: Photos by Lee Anne White

p. 64: Photos by (left) © Amy Rapaport; (right) ©James Wesley

p. 65: Photos by Lee Anne White

p. 65: Illustrations by Vincent Babak

pp. 66-69: Photos by Steve Aitken

pp. 71-73: Photos by Danielle Sherry

p. 74: Photos (top) courtesy Genevieve Schmidt; (bottom) Danielle Sherry

p. 75: Photos (top) courtesy Genevieve Schmidt; (bottom) Danielle Sherry

p. 76: Photos by Steve Aitken

p. 77: Photos by Danielle Sherry

p. 78: Photos by Michelle Gervais

p. 80: Photos by (top) Jennifer Brown; (middle) Michelle Gervais; (bottom) Jennifer Benner

p. 82: Photos by (top right and middle) Jennifer Brown; (bottom) Michelle Gervais

p. 83: Photos by Jennifer Benner

p. 84: Photos by (top left) Steve Aitken; (top right) Jennifer Benner; (bottom left) Michelle Gervais

p. 86-87: Illustrations by Carolyn Sumida & Joel Boulanger

p. 88-90: Photos by Todd Meier

p. 91: Photos by (top) Todd Meier; (bottom) Jennifer Benner

p. 92: Photos by (bottom left) © Ian Adams; (bottom right) Todd Meier

pp. 94-99: Photos by Daryl Beyers

pp. 100-105: Photos by Danielle Sherry

p. 102: Illustration by Grace S. McEnaney

p. 106: Photos by © Allan Mandell

p. 108: Photos by © C. Colston Burrell

p. 110: Photos by © Lauren Springer

p. 111: Photos by Lee Anne White

p. 112: Photos by Virgina Small

p. 114: Illustrations by Martha Garstang Hill

p. 116: Photos by © Sydney Eddison

p. 118: Photos by Todd Meier. Photo taken at Waterwise Garden, Bellevue Botanical Garden, designed by Stenn Design

p. 120: Photos by (bottom) Jennifer Benner; (top) Todd Meier. Photo taken at Waterwise Garden, Bellevue Botanical Garden, designed by Stenn Design.

p. 121: Photos by Virgina Small

p. 122: Photos by (top left and bottom left) © Amy Fahmy; (bottom right) Steve Silk

p. 123: Photos by © Amy Fahmy

p. 124: Photos by © Sydney Eddison

p. 125-126: Photos by Virgina Small

p. 127: Photos by (left) © Kathy Diemer; (right) Wendy Bowes

p. 128: Photos by (left) Virgina Small; (right) © Sydney Eddison

p. 129: Photos by (left) Wendy Bowes; (right) Virgina Small

p. 130: Photos by (left) Michael Gervais; (right) Virgina Small

p. 131: Photos by (left) Jennifer Benner; (right) Steve Silk

p. 132-133: Photos by Steve Aitken

p. 134: Illustration by Martha Garstang Hill

p.136-137: Photos by Brandi Spade

138-139: Photos by Steve Aitken

p. 140: Photos by Virgina Small

p. 142: Photos by Jennifer Benner

p. 143: Photos by Virgina Small

p. 144: Photos by Lee Anne White

p. 145: Photos by (top) Todd Meier; (bottom) Steve Aitken

p. 146: Photos by (top) Virgina Small; (bottom) Stephanie Fagan

p. 147: Photos by Melissa Lucas

p. 148-149: Line art by Andrew Schulman; Plantings by Melissa Lucas; Colorization by Steven Cominsky

p. 150-155: Photos by Virginia Small

pp. 156-163: Photos by Jennifer Benner

p. 164-169: Photos by Michelle Gervais

p. 170-171: Illustration by Beverley Colgan

p. 172: Photos by Jennifer Benner

p. 174: Photos by (left) Steve Aitken; (right) Michelle Gervais

p. 175: Photos by © Bill Johnson

p. 177: Photos by (top)Steve Aitken; (right) Michelle Gervais

pp. 178-181: Photos by Steve Silk

p. 180: Illustration by Mary Ellen Didion

pp. 182-185: Photos by Jennifer Brown

p. 186: Photos © Jacqueline Koch

p. 188: Photos by Jennifer Benner

p. 190: Photos courtesy Rebecca Sweet

p. 192: Photos by Michelle Gervais

p. 194: Photos by Todd Meier

p. 196: Photos by Michelle Gervais

p. 198: Photos courtesy Janie McCabe

p. 200: Photos courtesy Nancy Matthews

p. 202: Photos by Michelle Gervais

p. 204: Photos © Jacqueline Koch

p. 206: Photos by Michelle Gervais

INDEX